BAY AREA BIKE RIDES

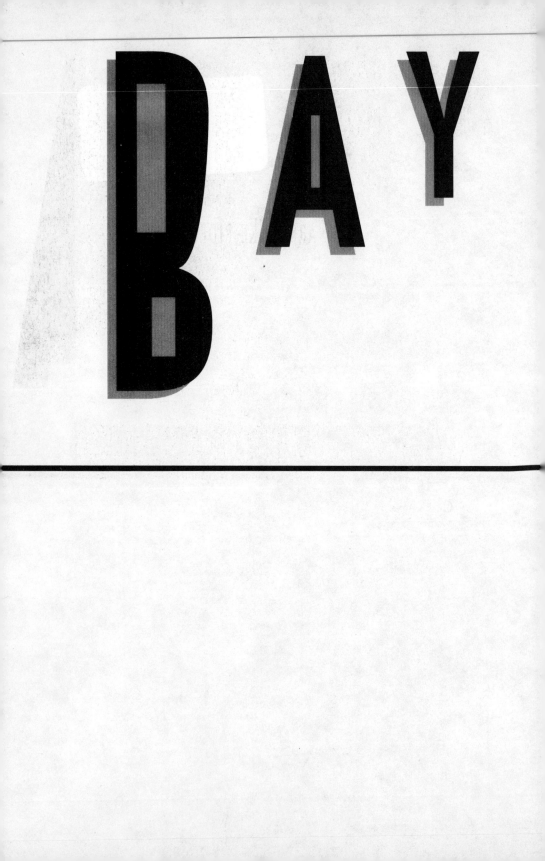

BAY

AREA

BIKE RIDES

COMPLETELY REVISED AND EXPANDED

By Ray Hosler

CHRONICLE BOOKS

SAN FRANCISCO

Second Edition

Library of Congress Cataloging-in-
Publication Data:

Hosler, Ray.
   Bay area bike rides : completely
revised and expanded / by Ray
Hosler.
      p. cm.
   Includes bibliographical references
(p.   ) and index.
   ISBN 0-8118-0612-X
   1. Bicycle touring–California–
San Francisco Bay Area–
Guidebooks. 2. San Francisco Bay
Area (Calif.)–Guidebooks.
I.Title.
GV1045.5.C22S264   1994
917.94'6–dc20

                    94–1051
                      CIP

Printed in theUnited States of
America.

Cover Illustration: John Hersey
Book Design: Robin Weiss

Distributed in Canada by Raincoast
Books, 8680 Cambie Street
Vancouver, B.C. V6P 6M9

10 9 8 7 6 5 4 3

Chronicle Books
85 Second Street
San Francisco, CA 94105

www.chroniclebooks.com

Table of Contents

Acknowledgments

A heartfelt thanks goes to the following individuals who helped me research, edit, and write *Bay Area Bike Rides:* Jobst Brandt, for leading the way on rides and giving editorial advice; Michael Kelley, for leading rides in the East Bay; Jim Westby, Ted Mock, Mark Levine, and others for riding along; Joe Breeze, for the Mt. Tamalpais mountain bike ride; John Schubert in Guerneville; Gage McKinney and Dick Wachs in San Jose; and all of the government agencies and libraries that provided invaluable information. Finally, a special thanks goes to Virginia Rich, my editor, for helping me get the names of roads right.

Introduction

Riding in the San Francisco Bay Area fulfills the dream of every bicyclist, as quiet country roads close to an urban setting reveal seemingly endless variety. Mountains, flatlands, cities, or rural parks—they're all nearby. It makes this venue, on the whole, the world's best bicycling location. After 15 years of bicycling here, I still find each ride a new adventure. And many an adventure I've had by bike: clambering over downed redwoods on Gazos Creek after the floods of 1982–83; riding into fluffy white fog and damp, cool canyons by the ocean on sweltering hot days; riding down the face of Mt. Diablo on a roller-coaster trail; seeing wild boar in remote sections of Henry W. Coe State Park; and moonlight rides over Dumbarton Bridge.

Although the Bay Area has its share of bad traffic, your bicycling experience can be car-free and carefree, if you take the rides I've mapped out here. Most rides in this book are within an hour's drive, and many can be reached by taking Bay Area Rapid Transit, a ferry, or a county bus. Consider the possibilities: Take the ferry from San Francisco to Sausalito, bicycle to Muir Woods National Monument. Stroll through the park's majestic redwood groves. Then cycle home over the inspiring Golden Gate Bridge, or return by ferry.

In the Bay Area, riding is a year-round activity. Each season has something to offer. In the spring I like to ride over Mt. Hamilton to see wildflowers. In the summer there's nothing more refreshing than a cool ride on the foggy Pacific Coast. In the fall, trees display crimson reds and golden yellow leaves in the remote reaches of the Santa Cruz Mountains. There's an invigorating scent of decaying leaves following the first rains. In the winter I often ride to the bay for bird-watching or visit local parks to hike.

Your bicycling pleasure will be enhanced if you're prepared to pay homage to the Bay Area's weather gods. Their moods change by the hour and by the mile, especially between bay and ocean and low and high elevations. It can be hot one minute and cold the next.

Even less predictable than the weather are motorists. Always be alert for sudden and unexpected maneuvers from cars. Never assume drivers know what you're doing either. Although car encounters are few and far between for most cyclists, remember you're not the only person using the road. Ride single file on all roads. You're better off avoiding confrontations with motorists. Unless you're looking for trouble, ignore rude or inattentive drivers.

No doubt, some roads that I've chosen here have changed or will change. They'll be rerouted, torn up, repaved, or even shut down. Since the first edition was published, the Bay Area has suffered a major earthquake, a devastating fire, and a seven-year drought that finally ended in 1993. That's why you should always check with a local bicycle shop about road conditions, especially if you're traveling some distance to a ride. The book's maps always include other interesting roads that you can take if you run into detours.

Off-road riding presents many of the same challenges as road riding, only you are the "motorist" on the trails and it's your responsibility to watch out for hikers and equestrians. Fortunately, off-road riding has gained credibility with park officials. Where we were banned from many parks five years ago, today we're welcomed. Be sure to check with a park ranger to see which trails are open to bicycles. We are still the new trail users. We must ride safely and responsibly, or trails will be closed again. Bicycles are permitted on narrow hiking trails in a few locations in the Bay Area. The "trails" shown in the off-road rides are mostly old logging or service roads designated for mixed use. Ride no faster than 15 mph and pass other trail users at reduced speed, usually 5 mph or less. But most important, have control of your bicycle at all times and be able to stop in a short distance. Note that Santa Clara County requires helmets be worn in some of its parks, and helmets are required on all Midpeninsula Regional Open Space District land.

The book is divided into three sections: mountain bike, road, and casual rides. Off-road rides take place on dirt, although you'll also be riding on pavement on many occasions. Road rides are completely on pavement. Casual rides are flat and located in parks and recreation areas where you can stay on recreation paths away from traffic. Use caution passing pedestrians, and don't exceed 10 mph when other trail users are present.

Usually it's best to take rides early in the morning on weekends to beat the crowds. If you start by 8:00 A.M., you'll avoid traffic, the air will be fresh and cool, and you'll finish your ride at a reasonable hour. Most stores open on Sunday by 9:00 A.M., in time for a food stop.

I've included some history that helps explain the origins of the roads you're riding on. Most of the Bay Area's rural roads were built between 1850 and 1890 for logging and commerce. The course chosen by the road builders sometimes followed trails used by the first Native Americans who settled here. Other roads were built for special purposes, like the road up Mt. Hamilton, which was constructed for the summit's telescope observatory. Parts of Highway 9 and Highway 236 were built in the early 1900s to connect Big Basin State Park with

Santa Clara Valley. More recently, recreation paths have emerged from railroad rights-of-way.

You will notice that many of the rides involve some climbing. With the proper gears and conditioning, most of the rides listed here can be accomplished by riders of all ages and abilities. In time you will realize that enjoyable riding, whether it be for scenery or to avoid traffic, is easy to find in the hills. If you're new to bicycling, you may want to start with casual rides and gradually increase your distance. Casual rides take place on flat terrain, so a terrain profile is not included. But when choosing a road ride or off-road ride, carefully study the terrain profile on the map to understand what to expect. Give yourself plenty of time to complete the ride, and don't forget to take food or money to buy a snack. Most of the routes pass at least one store or shopping center where you can get a bite to eat.

I wrote the book to include something for everyone. The longest ride is 104 miles, the shortest less than 4 miles. There are hilly, mountainous, and flat rides. Every ride was measured using an Avocet cyclometer, with all turns, rest stops, and points of interest noted in the Mileage Log. A cyclometer and mileage log will reduce the chance of getting lost. Enough said. Let's go for a bike ride.

Bicycles on Public Transit

Bicycles may be taken on BART, ferries, Amtrak, some buses, and light rail in the San Francisco Bay Area. Some restrictions apply and may change without notice, so check with the agencies listed here before using them.

Bay Area Rapid Transit (BART). Bike permit required. Travel restrictions during commute hours (you can travel in reverse commute directions on some lines during commute hours), but no restrictions on weekends, holidays, and non-commute hours. A three-year permit costs $3. Ask for a free three-week temporary permit at any primary station. For a five-page "Bikes on BART" brochure that describes the procedure and rules, and to purchase a permit, write to BART, 800 Madison Street, P.O. Box 12688, Oakland, CA 94604-2688. Phone (510) 464-7133 or 464-7135.

Joint Powers Board/Amtrak. Beginning September 1992, Amtrak allowed bicycles with permits during off-peak hours between San Francisco and San Jose. Up to four bikes are allowed on the first car, first come, first served. For a permit, write to JPB/Amtrak Bicycle Program, 45 North First Street, Suite 8300, San Jose, CA 95113-1295. Folding bicycles (folded and covered) allowed anytime. Phone (800) 660-4287.

Santa Clara County Transportation Agency. Bicycles (up to two per bus) are permitted on all buses in Santa Clara County, but only when there is room available and at the discretion of the driver. Operators cannot leave the bus to assist boarding. For more information, write to County Transit, Bikes on Route 300, P.O. Box 4009, Milpitas, CA 95035-2009. Attn: Commute Alternatives. Phone (408) 287-4210.

San Jose Light Rail. Extending from Santa Clara to southern San Jose, the light rail allows no more than two bicycles on the last car at the rear only. Phone (408) 321-2300.

Bay Ferry Service. All San Francisco Bay ferries servicing Sausalito, Larkspur, Tiburon, and Vallejo permit bicycles free. Golden Gate Transit operates ferries between the San Francisco Ferry Building and Sausalito and Larkspur seven days a week. The Larkspur ferry provides only commute service on weekdays. For information call (415) 453-2100, (415) 546-2896, or (800) 445-8800. The Red and White Fleet operates Monday through Friday between Sausalito and Tiburon and San Francisco's Ferry Building. Angel Island and Tiburon are serviced daily during the summer and on weekends and holidays during the winter. For information, call (415) 546-2815.

AC Transit (Alameda and Contra Costa Transit Authority). The T line bus crossing the San Francisco–Oakland Bay Bridge between San Francisco and Oakland and Alameda will carry up to four bicycles. It runs seven days a week, every half hour during the commute, otherwise hourly. There is also a Bay Bridge Bicycle Commuter Shuttle weekdays only. A 12-passenger van tows a trailer holding 12 bikes. Fee is $1. For information about the T line, call (510) 839-2882; for Commuter Shuttle, call (510) 464-0876.

SamTrans. San Mateo County buses permit bicycles, but only if the tires are removed and the chain is covered, and then only at the driver's discretion. For more information about bicycle organizations, bikes on Bay Area bridges, public bike lockers, and bicycles on public transit, contact the **Regional Bicycle Advisory Committee**, 3313 Grand Avenue, Oakland, CA 94610. Phone (510) 452-1221.

Bay Area Ride Locator Map

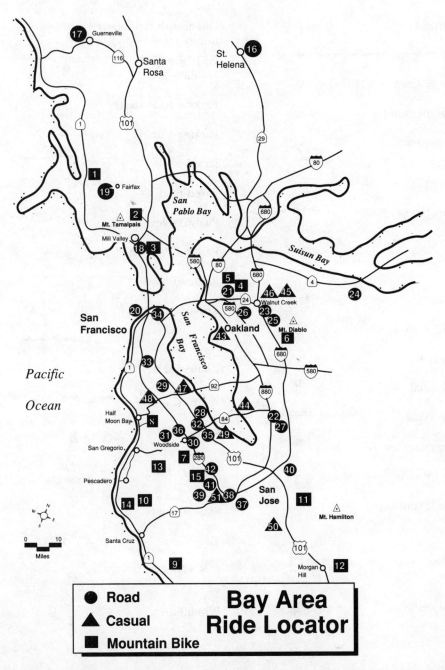

Key to Maps

Airport	✈	Old-growth redwoods/ unusual tree	🌲	
Altitude/point of interest	●	Park headquarters/ building	⚑ 🏠	
American Youth Hostel	🏠	**Parking (ride start)**	P	
Campground	▲	Parking (other)	ⓟ	
Compass	🧭	Paved path	〰	
Creek	············	Paved road	〰	
Dirt road or trail	〜	Picnic tables	🎋	
Ferry	⛴	Radar dish	📡	
Fort	⊥	Railroad tracks	┼┼┼┼┼	
Gate	●—●	Rock quarry	×	
Golf course	⛳	Route	➤	
Heliport	🚁	Route direction	▼	
Hospital	✚	Scale	▬ ▬	
Interstate	〰	School	🏫	
Interstate number	⑳⑧⓪	Slope rating	① -gradual ② -moderate ③ -steep	
Lighthouse	🗼	State highway	116	
Mountaintop	△	Town/city	○	
Observatory	🏛	U.S. highway	101	
Oil well	🗼	Windmill	🌬	

I. Mountain Bike Rides

1 Bolinas Ridge

Distance: *30 miles*
Terrain: *Moderately hilly*
Traffic: *Light to moderate for cars; bicyclists, hikers, equestrians*

One of the longer mountain bike rides in Marin County, and arguably the most scenic, runs the length of Bolinas Ridge. Midway through the ride the redwoods give way to a panoramic view. In the spring, when the grass is green, rolling fields bring to mind the *Sound of Music* and Julie Andrews singing in an Alpine meadow.

The ride starts in downtown Bolinas, although you may want to park elsewhere and ride into town. The quiet rural community likes its privacy. Every time Caltrans crews erect a Bolinas road sign, it's torn down.

Wildlife abounds in this lush valley formed by the San Andreas Fault. Nearby Bolinas Lagoon has some of the best bird viewing in the Bay Area. And mature eucalyptus lining Olema Bolinas Road shelter the migratory monarch butterfly during the winter.

After crossing Highway 1, begin a moderately steep climb on the lightly traveled Fairfax Bolinas Road. You'll see Bolinas Lagoon and the ocean below. Turn left at the summit, where there's a steel gate marking Bolinas Ridge Trail. In wet weather, slippery tree roots make the first half-mile

Mileage Log

0.0 Start mileage in Bolinas at intersection of Brighton Avenue and Olema Bolinas Road.

0.8 Right at stop sign, staying on Olema Bolinas Road.

1.9 Right at unmarked intersection, staying on Olema Bolinas Road.

2.0 Straight at Highway 1 stop sign to Fairfax Bolinas Road 6.3 Summit. Bolinas Ridge Trail on left at gate. 9.6 McCurdy Trail on left; goes to Highway 1; legal for bicycles. 11.2 Randall Trail on left; goes to Highway 1. Legal for bicycles. 12.2 Shafter Bridge Trail on right. 12.6 Gate; 14.0 Gate; 14.3 Gate; 15.0 Gate.

Bolinas Ridge Trail overlooks Tomales Bay in the distance.

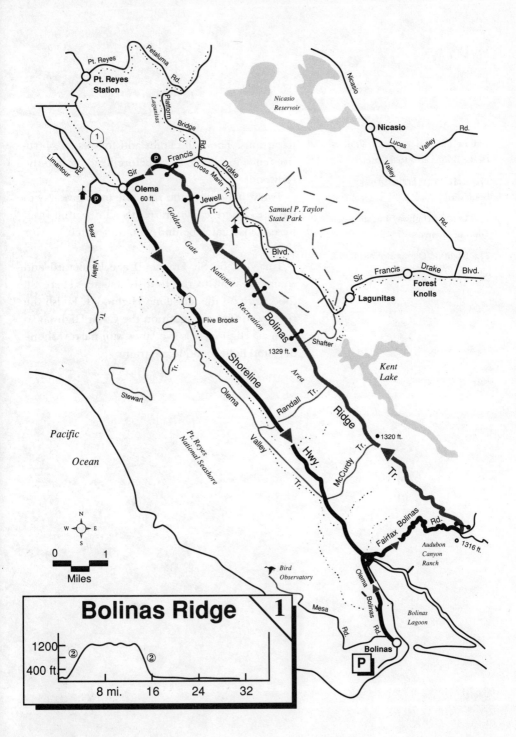

Pt. Reyes

**Pt. Reyes
Station**

Petaluma Rd.

Lagunitas

Platform Bridge Rd.

*Nicasio
Reservoir*

Nicasio

Nicasio

Lucas Valley Rd.

Valley

Rd.

Cr.

Limantour Rd.

1

Sir Francis Drake

P

Olema
60 ft.

Cross Marin Tr.

*Samuel P. Taylor
State Park*

Jewell Tr.

Bear Valley Tr.

Golden

Gate

National

Recreation

Bolinas

Blvd.

Sir Francis Drake Blvd.

Lagunitas

**Forest
Knolls**

1

Five Brooks

Area

1329 ft.

Shafter Tr.

*Kent
Lake*

Shoreline

Stewart Tr.

Olema

Randall Tr.

Ridge

1320 ft.

*Pacific

Ocean*

*Pt. Reyes
National Seashore*

Valley

Tr.

Hwy.

McCurdy Tr.

Tr.

1316 ft.

Fairfax Bolinas Rd.

*Audubon
Canyon
Ranch*

N
W E
S

0   1
Miles

*Bird
Observatory*

Mesa

Rd.

Olema Bolinas Rd.

*Bolinas
Lagoon*

Bolinas

P

Bolinas Ridge

1

1200
400 ft.

② ②

8 mi.   16   24   32

16.0 Left at Y in trail to Sir Francis Drake Boulevard. 16.2 Gate.

17.4 Left on Sir Francis Drake Boulevard.

18.5 Left on Highway 1 at stop sign. Town of Olema.

27.6 Right on Olema Bolinas Road.

29.6 End ride in Bolinas.

hazardous. The trail climbs and follows an obtrusive fence for a mile or so before heading into the redwoods.

Twelve miles into the ride, the trees give way to pastures where cattle graze. It's all downhill from here. Close gates behind you, and watch out for cattle.

Turn left on Sir Francis Drake Boulevard and zoom downhill to the town of Olema. There's a food store on the left along Highway 1. Finish the ride by continuing south on the Coast Highway to Bolinas. Highway 1 is two lanes with narrow shoulders and light to moderate traffic.

Mountain Bike Rides

2 Lake Lagunitas

Distance: 9 miles
Terrain: Hilly
Traffic: Hikers, equestrians, bicyclists

Mileage Log

0.0 Start mileage at post office on Ross Common in Ross, off Sir Francis Drake Boulevard. Ride west a short distance and turn left onto Lagunitas Drive.

0.8 Lagunitas Drive ends at Natalie Coffin Greene Park.

1.1 Right in parking lot at wooden bridge. Sign on other side of bridge points way to Mt. Tamalpais and Phoenix Lake.

1.4 Straight at junction. Phoenix Lake dam on left. Restrooms on right. 1.5 Worn Spring Road junction. Keep left.

2.1 Four-way junction. Go straight uphill on Fish Grade. (Shaver Grade on right. Eldridge Grade on left. You'll return on Eldridge Grade.) 2.7 Pavement. End of steep climb. South Marin Line Grade on left.

2.8 Left at Sky Oaks Road. Bon Tempe Lake.

3.1 Parking area and picnic grounds for Lake Lagunitas. Restrooms and phone on left. Take dirt road with sign that says Protection Road. 3.2 Cross dam.

3.4 Left at junction. Circle lake. Sign says Rock Spring Road.

4.3 Right on Lakeview Road. 4.6 Meadow.

The Marin Municipal Water District has one of the most enlightened land use policies of any Bay Area water district. They permit bicycling on land surrounding the district's sparkling blue reservoirs, which make up the Mt. Tamalpais watershed. Three of the five reservoirs are within easy riding distance of the town of Ross—Phoenix, Bon Tempe, and Lagunitas. You'll see these reservoirs as you ride on water department service roads in the wooded hills above Ross.

Lagunitas was built in 1873 by William T. Coleman, who needed water to build housing for San Rafael. Phoenix was built in 1905 and Bon Tempe in 1949. Marin County residents draw almost all their water from these reservoirs.

Start riding from city park in downtown Ross. On the way to Natalie Coffin Greene Park at the end of Lagunitas Road, you'll pass stately homes on streets lined with liquidambar and Dutch elm. In the fall the street looks more like New England than sunny California. Pick up Phoenix Trail behind a gate in the parking lot. After a quarter-mile of easy climbing, you'll reach Phoenix Lake.

Stay on Phoenix Trail until you reach the intersection with Eldridge Grade on the left and Shaver Grade on the right. Continue straight on Fish Grade. It's a hustle in low gear until the dirt road levels at a paved service road that intersects Sky Oaks Road at the summit. Bon Tempe Lake is straight ahead.

Turn left on Sky Oaks and ride to Lake Lagunitas parking area. Climb a dirt road on the left to reach Lagunitas Dam. Cross a wooden platform on the other side of the dam. Ride counterclockwise around the lake, keeping left at junctions. The southern shore has a level section of

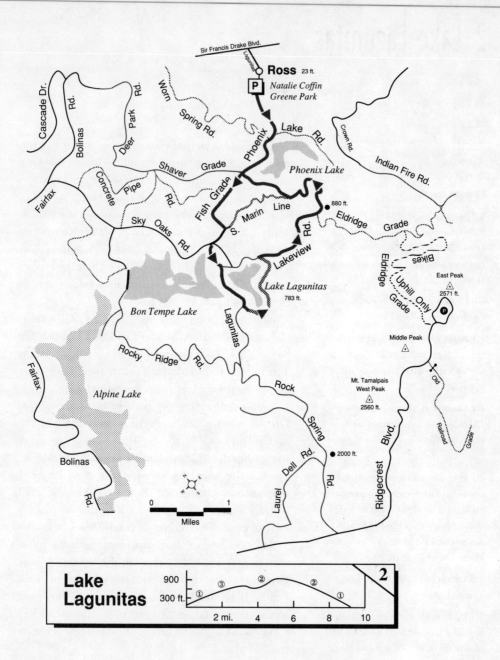

Sir Francis Drake Blvd.

Ross 23 ft.

P
Natalie Coffin Greene Park

Cascade Dr.

Bolinas Rd.

Fairfax

Worn

Deer Park Rd.

Spring Rd.

Phoenix Lake Rd.

Crown Rd.

Indian Fire Rd.

Shaver Grade

Concrete

Pipe Rd.

Sky Oaks Rd.

Fish Grade

Phoenix

Phoenix Lake

S. Marin Line

880 ft.

Eldridge Grade

Lakeview Rd.

Bikes

Uphill Only

Eldridge Grade

East Peak
△
2571 ft.

P

Bon Tempe Lake

Lagunitas

Lake Lagunitas
783 ft.

Middle Peak
△

Fairfax

Rocky Ridge Rd.

Alpine Lake

Rock Spring

Mt. Tamalpais
West Peak
△
2560 ft.

Old

Bolinas

Laurel Dell Rd.

Rd.

2000 ft.

Ridgecrest Blvd.

Railroad Grade

0   1
Miles

N
W   E
S

**Lake
Lagunitas**

900

300 ft.

① ③ ② ② ①

2 mi.   4   6   8   10

2

5.0 Left on Eldridge Grade Trail.

5.7 Left at junction, downhill.

6.2 Right, downhill on Eldridge Grade, at Marin Line Grade.

7.0 Right on Fish Grade–Phoenix Lake Trail.

9.0 Right at Ross Common.

9.1 End ride at starting point.

road in the woods and fords two small streams. Leaving the lakeshore, you turn right on Lakeview Road and climb Eldridge Grade.

You'll circle back to the major trail intersection you passed earlier. Eldridge's gradual descent lets you enjoy the views of Richardson Bay and San Francisco. You'll come to a crucial junction about a mile down Eldridge. Take the right fork; the left fork goes up to Sky Oaks Road.

The water district restricts bicycles to fire roads. The district's speed limit is 15 mph, and regulations require slowing to 5 mph to pass other trail users.

If you want to ride to the Mt. Tamalpais summit from Eldridge Grade, take the right fork from Lakeview Road. Bicycles are not permitted to ride down Eldridge, so have an alternate route prepared. Marin County Water District maps can be obtained by sending a stamped, self-addressed envelope to Bicycle Trails Council of Marin, P.O. Box 13842, San Rafael, CA 94913-3842. Phone (415) 479-5482.

3 Mt. Tamalpais

Distance: 22 miles
Terrain: Hilly
Traffic: Light for cars; hikers, bicyclists

Mileage Log

0.0 Start mileage directly under Richardson Bay Bridge, Highway 101. Parking is available next to the bridge off Pohono Street. Ride north on recreation path. Sections of path may flood at high tide. 0.1 Cross bridge over Coyote Creek inlet.

0.5 Left at crosswalk, then immediate right onto Miller Avenue in bike lane. 1.1 Camino Alto stoplight. Tamalpais High School on left.

2.1 Right on Millwood at green bike route sign, followed by immediate left on Presidio Avenue. Right on Forest.

2.3 Left on East Blithedale Avenue at stop sign.

2.5 Straight on West Blithedale Avenue.

2.8 Keep left.

3.6 Right at Blithedale Summit Gate, beginning Old Railroad Grade.

3.8 Straight at junction.

4.4 Left at junction, downhill. Former site of Horseshoe Bend Trestle. 5.1 McKinley Cut. Rock was blasted to lay track. Named for President McKinley, who visited this site.

Marin County is mountain bike country. As you ride on the Old Railroad Grade up Mt. Tamalpais, you'll understand why the modern mountain bike was invented here. Creators Joe Breeze, Gary Fisher, Charlie Kelly, and Otis Guy lived at the base of the mountain when they started riding one-speed clunkers, first downhill and later both directions after gears were added. Within a decade, the mountain bike had progressed from a one-speed clunker to a technologically sophisticated multi-geared wonder. Joe Breeze is recognized as the first frame builder to make the modern mountain bike, in 1977.

Many trails and roads lead to the railroad grade, which snakes its way up the mountain in 281 curves. This tour starts in Marin City at a parking lot under Highway 101. You'll ride north through Mill Valley, pick up the railroad grade to West Point, head to the ocean, and return on Highway 1 by Tennessee Valley in the Golden Gate National Recreation Area.

The railroad grade is popular with hikers and bicyclists year-round. The speed limit is 15 mph, 5 mph when passing other trail users.

About the only visible remnant of the railroad is a concrete platform called Mesa Junction Station, 6.8 miles into the ride, at the junction to Muir Woods. Farther up, there was another water tower. You can still get a drink from its source at Fern Canyon Falls.

West Point Inn, established in 1904, lies at an important trail junction. (It's about a mile and a half to the summit, where there's a concession stand that's usually open in the summer.) Keep left at West Point and go to Pan Toll Station to pick up the Coastal Fire Trail. The trail descends to

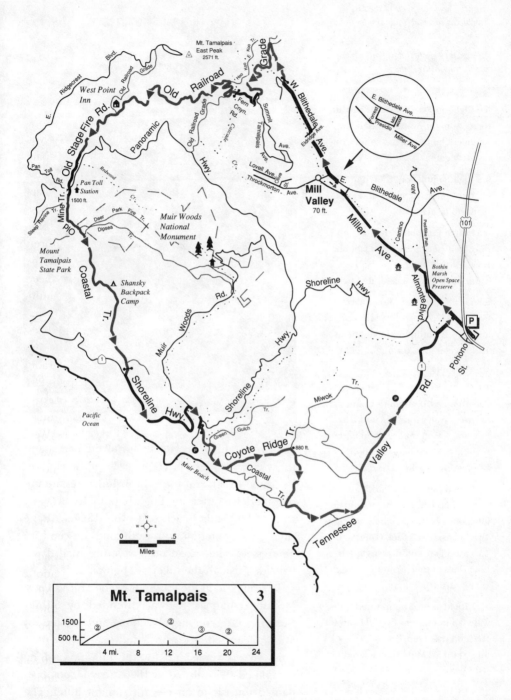

Right: The gentle slope of the Mt. Tamalpais railroad grade invites family riding.

Opposite: Coyote Ridge Trail climbs steeply from Muir Beach.

5.6 Right on Fern Canyon Road at top of Summit Avenue, paved. 6.2 Pavement ends; railroad grade continues at gate.

6.5 Right at junction, then immediate right again. Remains of railroad platform on left.

6.9 Left at junction with Hoo-Koo-E-Koo Trail (second bend of Double Bow Knot). 8.0 Fern Canyon Falls. Train water tower was located here.

8.8 Left to Old Stage Road. West Point Inn. To reach Mt. Tam summit, go right. Water fountain at junction. 10.4 Pavement. Continue straight. Water fountain.

10.9 Cross Panoramic Highway to Pan Toll park headquarters and parking area. Water fountain and restrooms. Continue west on paved road. 11.2 Maintenance station. Begin Old Mine Road, dirt.

11.4 Keep right. Deer Park Fire Road junction on left. 11.5 Keep right at junction. 12.5 Keep right at junction. 12.8 Shansky Backpack Camp on left. 13.5 Steel gate and flower garden both sides of trail. Continue straight. Do not disturb flowers.

13.7 Right at two round wood posts with gap in fence to Coast Highway. Descend past Muir Beach Overlook on right. 15.2 Muir Woods Road on left.

15.4 Right at Pacific Way. Pelican Inn on corner.

15.6 Left at aluminum gate next to bridge over creek.

Highway 1 and gives you a view of the ocean and rocky cliffs. Go left on Highway 1 and descend to Redwood Creek and the Pelican Inn, a restaurant-bar modeled after an English pub. It's a steep climb from Muir Beach to Coyote Ridge. At the ridge trail junction, go right and descend to Tennessee Valley Road on a wide fire road. It's a flat ride through the valley to Highway 1.

The railroad grade was built by the Mill Valley & Mount Tamalpais Railway, founded by Sidney Cushing. Overcoming objections and lawsuits by Mill Valley residents, who didn't like having their quiet streets ripped up for the railway, Cushing completed the railroad in 1896. Shay locomotives hauled tourists to an elegant summit hotel. The railroad became a popular tourist attraction, but hardly a financial success. It weathered the lean years and even extended its line to Muir Woods

15.9 Left at Muir Beach Lagoon junction. Right at next junction up steep hill on dirt road, 200 yards from gate. (Left goes to Green Gulch Farm and Zen Center.) 16.4 Coastal Trail on right.

16.7 Right at gate and continue straight up steep hill.

17.2 Right at junction on top of Coyote Ridge. Right again in 100 yards on dirt road. 18.6 Coastal Trail on right.

19.2 Left at bottom of hill in Tennessee Valley. Pavement begins in 0.3 miles. 19.9 Miwok Stables and parking lot.

21.5 Left under bridge at Highway 1 and Tennessee Valley Road junction. At gravel parking lot on left, take trail under bridge (floods at high tide), which becomes paved recreation path back to start of ride.

21.7 Left at first junction and then right on recreation path that returns to starting point.

21.8 End ride.

with gravity cars. Automobiles, buses, and the Great Depression spelled doom for the railroad. Ridgecrest Boulevard to the Mt. Tamalpais summit was completed in 1924. The railroad shut down for good in 1929 after a fire swept the mountain, destroying the hotel and a locomotive. A year later the rails were removed and the right-of-way turned over to hikers.

4 Briones Regional Park

Distance: 15 miles
Terrain: Hilly and steep in spots
Traffic: Hikers, equestrians, bicyclists

Mileage Log

0.0 Start mileage at the Bear Creek entrance to Briones Regional Park off Bear Creek Road. The parking lot is about a half-mile from Bear Creek Road. Ride north on Abrigo Valley Trail.

0.9 Left at junction with Mott Peak Trail. 1.4 Maud Walen Camp on right.

1.9 Right on Briones Crest Trail.

2.2 Right at Lagoon Trail junction, staying on Briones Crest Trail.

3.0 Left on Lagoon Trail.

3.6 Right on Toyon Canyon Trail.

4.6 Left on Pine Tree Trail.

4.7 Right on Orchard Trail. 5.3 Cross Old Briones Road at Rancho Briones.

5.9 Right on Alhambra Creek Trail at Alhambra Creek Valley Staging Area. Drinking fountain and restrooms.

6.9 Left onto Spengler Trail.

7.9 Keep right at junction with Blue Oak Trail.

8.7 Left at junction, staying on Spengler Trail.

10.0 Right onto Spengler Trail. Dirt road goes to service area.

10.4 Right on Table Top Trail.

11.1 Left on Briones Crest Trail.

Briones Regional Park, an island of open space surrounded by country estates and ranches, gives the East Bay mountain biker plenty of excitement close to home. Almost all the old ranch roads winding through the park, shown as hiking trails on park maps, are open for bicycling. Volunteer trail work and participation in park meetings by the Coast Range Riders has helped keep the park open for bicycling.

In the spring, on secluded hilltops, there's a hint of the green hills of Ireland. The park has enough variety—wide valleys, high ridges, and deep canyons—to make mountain biking fun for riders of all abilities.

This hilly ride is one of many options for covering all corners of the park's 5,000 acres. Several climbs are "walls" that require walking, even by "mountain goat riders" with extra-low gears.

Most trails are marked at intersections, but with so many junctions it's easy to miss a turn. Trails vary from wide dirt roads to grassy paths. In the spring, cattle that graze inside the park can turn some trail sections into quagmires. Sometimes it's hard to tell the cattle paths from the trails.

Begin riding from the Bear Creek Road staging area, where there's a water fountain and restroom. Ride north from the parking lot on Abrigo Valley Trail, and begin a steady climb through a wooded canyon with a stream. The road takes you to a valley and lush meadow that has a picnic area at Wee-Ta-Chi Camp, a tranquil setting protected by giant bay trees.

The trail turns narrow and steep beyond the camp. After a hairpin turn, you'll come to a ridge with a grand view of Mt. Diablo, Benicia Martinez Bridge, Mt. Tamalpais, and Mt. St. Helena to the north.

Mountain Bike Rides

Briones Regional Park 4

1200
400 ft.

② ② ③ ① ③

3 mi. 6 9 12 15

0 .75
Miles

N
W E
S

12.0 **Right** at junction.

12.1 **Left** on Briones Crest Trail.

12.6 **Left** on Mott Peak Trail.

13.0 **Left** on Black Oak Trail.

14.0 **Right** on Old Briones Road.

14.8 Ride ends at Bear Creek parking lot.

As you descend Briones Crest Trail, you'll see two small ponds. Sindicich Lagoon on Lagoon Trail is fenced to keep out cattle. There's a long bumpy descent on Toyon Canyon Trail and Pine Tree Trail, named for the trees that grow here. Orchard Trail is the site of a former orchard and ranch. Coulter pine, with its huge cones more than a foot long and weighing two pounds, grows near the orchard.

Cross the paved Old Briones Road and descend to a wide valley, where you'll find the Alhambra

Briones Crest Trail overlooks large areas of Briones Regional Park.

Creek Valley Staging Area. Follow Alhambra Creek Trail up a valley that's cloaked in blue lupine in the spring. There's a steady climb through oaks and bay laurels. On Spengler Trail you'll climb through a beautiful stand of oaks. After a descent, climb the first wall, about 200 yards long. Turn left and stay on Spengler Trail. You'll see ranch houses in the canyon below. Drop into a gully and assault the next wall to a ridge, where there's more climbing.

Take a hard right at a gate to join Table Top Trail. After a roller-coaster hill, you'll pass a communications tower. In the spring you'll find a meadow thick with poppies. To the right, there's a panorama of Suisun Bay, and on a clear day you can see the Sierra. Most of the climbing is over now. Table Top intersects Briones Crest Trail. Ride down to Lagoon Trail, climb the hill you rode down earlier, and take a left onto Mott Peak Trail, which runs along a narrow ridge and over Mott Peak at 1,424 feet. Descend Black Oak Trail and hold onto your helmet for a steep, bumpy descent to Old Briones Road. Turn right and ride back to the Bear Creek Staging Area.

Briones Regional Park opened in 1967. Prior to becoming a park, the land was used for cattle grazing. It was left undeveloped as San Pablo Dam watershed. The earliest settler was Felipe Briones, who built a home in 1829 near the Bear Creek entrance. His land was part of the huge Rancho Boca de la Cañada del Pinole Mexican land grant. During Prohibition the East Bay's isolated ranchlands became bootlegging hideouts. For more information, phone the East Bay Regional Park District (510) 531-9300.

Mountain Bike Rides

5 Mt. Diablo Off-road

Distance: 19 miles
Terrain: Steep and rocky
Traffic: Hikers, equestrians, bicyclists, cattle

Mileage Log

0.0 Start mileage at gate beginning Mitchell Canyon Trail at the far end of Juniper Campground. The campground is on the left, 2.4 miles from the ranger station junction. Parking is available at the campground or at the overlook.

0.4 Left at junction to begin Burma Road. 0.5 Gate.

1.3 Right at unsigned junction. Spring.

2.4 Left, downhill at junction. Called Upper Gate Road on wooden sign, Burma Road on maps. 3.2 Acorn Flat.

3.5 Right, downhill on Burma Road at unsigned junction of Angel Kerley Road. 3.6 and 3.7 **Extremely** steep downhill.

4.0 Cross North Gate Road at gates on both sides.

4.5 Left, downhill at unmarked junction.

4.8 Right at Pine Pond onto Stage Road. You'll ford Pine Creek 10 times. 5.6 Park boundary and gate. Keep right on dirt road.

6.4 Right, downhill at junction. Old reservoir and spillway on right. 6.5 Gate. Continue straight. 6.7 Gate into Castle Rock Park. Sign says No Public Access, but it's open to public. Begin

Off-road bike riding wasn't permitted in Mt. Diablo State Park until 1990. The tireless efforts of Michael Kelley and the Bicycle Trails Council of the East Bay helped convince park officials that it was the right thing to do. Now many miles of "trails" are open. In reality, it's many miles of dirt roads. Most narrow trails are not open for bicycling.

You'll begin the ride high on the mountain at 2,880 feet and take a breathtaking plunge to the lowest points in the park. Few rides in the Bay Area have such uncompromising views. From the bald mountainside you can see the Golden Gate Bridge and the Sacramento River Delta. The topography is so dramatic here that the roads and valleys below look more like roller coasters than places you would ride a bike. At the junction of Mitchell Canyon Road and Burma Road, you'll see to your right, far below, a steep canyon and a rock quarry carved into the mountainside like an open wound. Burma Road descends steeply (most of the park's dirt roads have steep sections) after rounding a corner, although not so steeply that bike control is difficult. Be sure to keep right at the junction, where there's a water tank and spring.

The road flattens at Acorn Flat and then goes up a short, steep hill. Burma Road continues along the side of a ridge, crossing several streams that flow in the spring. The real "fun" comes at the Angel Kerley Road junction, where there are two vertical plunges of at least 50 yards each. They are extremely steep! The dropoffs appear suddenly, as Burma Road disappears beneath you.

Beyond North Gate Road, the gradients turn decidedly less aggressive. You'll descend a short distance to the reed-filled Pine Pond, where

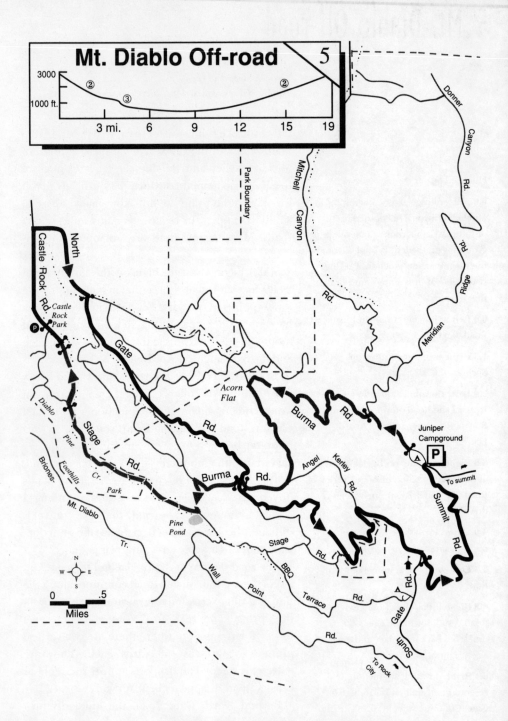

Mt. Diablo Off-road

5

3000

1000 ft.

② ③ ②

3 mi. 6 9 12 15 19

Park Boundary

Donner Canyon Rd.

Mitchell Canyon Rd.

Meridian Ridge Rd.

Castle Rock Rd.

North Gate Rd.

Castle Rock Park

P

Acorn Flat

Burma Rd.

Juniper Campground

P

To summit

Diablo

Pine

Briones

Foothills

Stage Rd.

Cr. Park

Mt. Diablo Tr.

Burma Rd.

Pine Pond

Angel

Kerley Rd.

Summit Rd.

Rd.

Stage

BBQ

Wall Point

Terrace Rd.

Rd.

Gate Rd.

South

To Rock City

N
W E
S

0 .5

Miles

Mt. Diablo's Burma Road descends the steep western slope.

pavement. Park has water, bathrooms. 7.1 Gate. Parking.

8.8 Right on North Gate Road. 10.1 Park entrance. 13.0 Burma Road.

16.5 Straight, uphill at park headquarters junction on North Gate Road, which becomes Summit Road.

18.8 End ride at Juniper Campground. 2.2 miles to Mt. Diablo summit.

red-winged blackbirds perform their raucous mating rituals in the spring. If you like fording streams, Stage Road has to be the best stretch of off-road riding around, as the road crosses Pine Creek 10 times. The best riding is in the spring when the water is running. However, the road turns to mud in wet weather.

Even on dry days in the spring, the trail has muddy sections hemmed in by poison oak. Finally you'll reach an empty reservoir and spillway. There's a short descent to a gate and then another gate that brings you into Castle Rock Park. Many equestrians use the trail, so ride carefully and always stop to let equestrians pass. Continue through the park, and you'll soon reach a paved road that takes you to the North Gate Road junction.

Take North Gate Road back to the starting point. It's a 9-mile climb with a steady grade. Bring your sunscreen on sunny days. For an easier ride, do the lower section of this figure-eight loop. Although Mt. Diablo is not a volcano, after this ride, you'll know what it's like to ride down one.

6 Tilden and Wildcat Canyon Regional Parks

Distance: 16 miles
Terrain: Hilly
Traffic: Bicyclists, hikers, equestrians

Mileage Log

0.0 Start mileage at Lone Oak picnic area (drinking fountain) off Central Park Drive. Ride south on Meadow Canyon Trail, uphill.

1.4 Right, downhill on Curran Trail.

2.0 Right on Wildcat Gorge Trail, downhill.

2.8 Return to Lone Oak picnic area. Begin riding to right and north on pavement, which becomes Loop Trail. 3.0 Gate. 3.9 Jewel Lake on left. 4.6 Gate. Entering Wildcat Canyon Regional Park.

5.9 Trail junction for Havey Canyon, Conlon, and Rifle Range Road trails. Go straight. 6.1 Mezue Trail junction and cattle guard. 6.9 Old parking lot.

7.6 Right on Belgum Trail, uphill. Gate at 7.7.

8.5 Keep left at Y intersection. Bottom of hill at 8.7. Begin climb-walk up No Way Hill. 8.8 Summit. 9.3 Second summit with great view. 9.8 Mezue Trail junction. Keep left around corral. 10.1 Gate. 10.2 Begin paved Nimitz Way. Nike missile pad on left. 10.6 Havey Canyon Trail junction. 11.9 Conlon Trail on right.

14.2 Inspiration Point. **Right** on Curran Trail, then right again on Meadow Canyon Trail.

15.7 Ride ends at Lone Oak picnic area.

Tilden and Wildcat Canyon Regional Parks offer the "wild life" for mountain bike riders. They're also protected habitats for plants and animals and the last parcels of open space in the East Bay hills. But to keep cyclists from getting carried away in their enjoyment, park rangers and volunteers from the Bicycle Trails Council of the East Bay closely monitor off-road riding. Trails Council members have volunteered thousands of hours of their time monitoring and repairing trails and helping with other activities. Thanks to their efforts, cyclists may ride on most fire roads and service roads in the parks, unless otherwise posted. Bicycles are not permitted on narrow hiking trails. The map shows only those trails open to bicycles.

The tour begins in Tilden Regional Park and makes a short loop with a long climb and descent. A much larger loop through Wildcat Canyon Regional Park follows. You'll climb to the park's highest point and return on Nimitz Way.

Begin riding up Meadow Canyon Trail to Curran Trail, which goes into a narrow canyon through eucalyptus and redwoods. Note the caves on the west canyon wall. Turn right and take Wildcat Gorge Trail through riparian habitat, kept moist by springs that run year-round. Willows grow close to the trail. The trail is closed to bicycles during the wet season.

Return to the start at Lone Oak picnic area, keep right, and go north on a paved road that turns to dirt beyond a gate marking the Loop Trail. The wide road takes you through a eucalyptus grove and into Wildcat Canyon. Jewel Lake on the left is part of the Tilden Nature Area, where biologists study the 740-acre parcel. Bicycles are allowed only on Loop Trail.

Mountain Bike Rides

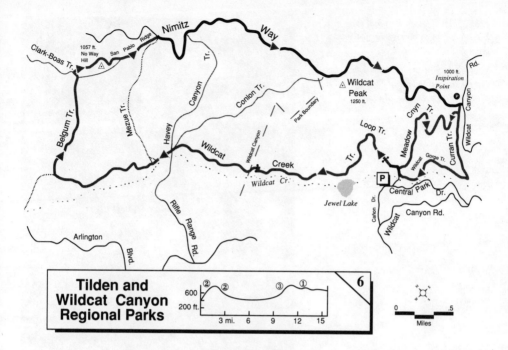

In Wildcat Canyon Regional Park you'll see hill-sides covered with the brilliant purple and red flowers of thistles. With their large seed pods, these plants evoke images from *Invasion of the Body Snatchers*. In the movie, giant podlike plants containing aliens are sent to Earth to "occupy" human bodies. The invasion here is no less serious. Thistles flourish where land has been overgrazed by cattle. The plants are difficult to eradicate, and they spread quickly.

Leaving the thistle, you'll ride across an old parking lot that washed out during the winter floods of 1982–83. In less than a mile, turn right on Belgum Trail, which presents a steep climb to Clark Boas Trail. The trail has more thistle and a palm grove marking where a home once stood.

Keep left at the Clark-Boas junction and ride around "No Way Hill" to the north face, where you'll find a dirt road that goes up at more than a 20-percent grade. Another steep climb takes you to a knoll. You're rewarded with a view of the park and San Francisco, San Pablo, and Suisun bays.

San Pablo Ridge Trail joins Nimitz Way. Nearby concrete bunkers are missile silos, abandoned in

Loop Trail in Tilden Regional Park near Jewel Lake passes through a eucalyptus grove.

Low gears will come in handy when climbing the summit following No Way Hill in Wildcat Canyon Regional Park.

the 1960s. Nimitz Way hugs a ridgetop that extends to Inspiration Point and beyond. Take Curran Trail on the right at the gate, ride a short distance downhill, and go right at Meadow Canyon Trail, returning to the Lone Oak picnic area.

Tilden Regional Park was named for Major Charles Lee Tilden, a park founder and first president of the East Bay Regional Park District's board of directors. It is one of three original regional parks established in 1936.

7 Alpine Road

Distance: 16 miles
Terrain: Long hills, steep descent
Traffic: Light for cars; bicyclists, hikers, equestrians

Mileage Log

0.0 Start mileage on Portola Valley Road at the Portola Valley Town Center sign on the west side of the road. Look for an old red schoolhouse, now called the Valley Art Gallery. 0.5 Note exit point for Windy Hill at dirt road on right, before the white guardrail.

1.4 Right on Alpine Road at stop sign. 4.7 Green gate. Ride around on path at left or lift bike over gate. 4.8 Corte Madera Creek bridge. 5.3 Mud turn (muddy when wet). 6.1 Crazy Pete's Road on right.

7.3 Right on Page Mill Road at green gate.

8.0 Right on Skyline Boulevard at stop sign. 8.5 Top of hill. 8.8 Begin 1.2-mile descent. 9.1 Vista point. 9.8 Crazy Pete's Road on right. 10.7 Fogerty Winery. 12.9 Windy Hill parking.

13.3 Right on Spring Ridge Road at gate. Begin descent.

14.7 Left at junction.

15.8 Right at gate on dirt road.

15.9 Left on Portola Road.

16.4 End ride at Portola Valley town hall.

Alpine Road attracts so many riders that you can call it a "mountain bike boulevard." The road is popular for its steady grade and easy access from nearby Peninsula cities. San Mateo County built Alpine Road to bring commerce from Santa Cruz County while bypassing Santa Clara County. The county still maintains the right-of-way, but Midpeninsula Regional Open Space District (MROSD) owns most of the land around the road. The road was closed to car traffic in the late 1960s.

Over the years, the road's condition has varied from excellent to impassable. Heavy rains in the mid-1980s caused a landslide near the start of the dirt road, dissuading most cyclists from using the route. Local cyclists built a narrow trail through the slide, and further improved the road by cleaning culverts and filling ruts. In the winter of 1989, San Mateo County graded the road, uncovering a long-forgotten bridge over Corte Madera Creek.

Start your ride in Portola Valley at a small shopping center. Ride south on Portola Road, and turn right on Alpine Road at the stop sign. The narrow road is paved for several miles. The dirt starts at a green gate next to a driveway.

At Page Mill Road go right and continue to Skyline Boulevard; turn right again at the stop sign. It's mostly downhill to Spring Ridge Road, which starts as a poorly marked trail. Aim for a prominent grove of cypress in a meadow. The trees were planted in 1888 as a wind shelter for a house built here by Willington Orton. The house was torn down in 1934.

You'll be riding down Windy Hill. Poor soil and constant movement of the subsoil have stifled tree growth. Windy Hill was given its name in the 1960s by the U.S. Geological Survey. It was originally

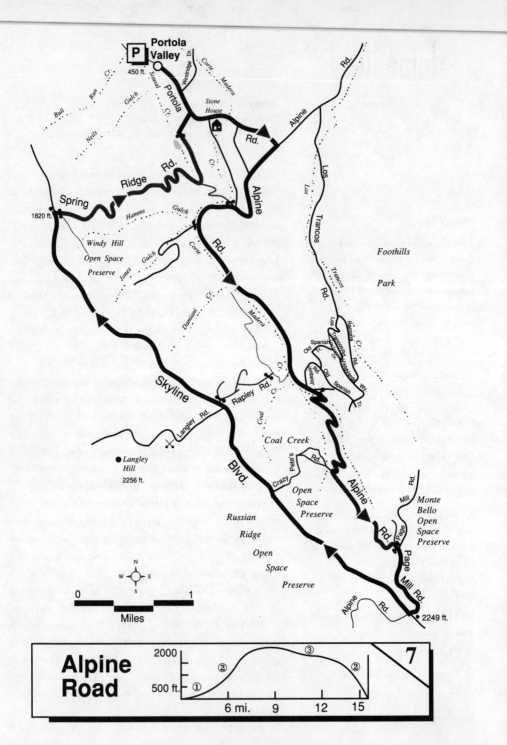

Alpine Road

7

called Spring Hill, for its many springs, but Windy Hill became a popular name, because it is indeed windy.

Mountain Bike Rides

8 Purisima Creek Road

Distance: 21 miles
Terrain: Hilly
Traffic: Light to moderate for cars; bicyclists, hikers, equestrians

Mileage Log

0.0 Start mileage at the Midpeninsula Regional Open Space District parking lot on Skyline Boulevard, 2.4 miles north of Kings Mountain Road in San Mateo County. Leave parking lot and go west on trail.

0.3 Left on hiking trail at four-way junction. Unsigned.

0.9 Right on Harkins Fire Trail. Begin steep descent.

3.1 Keep right at junction near Purisima Creek.

3.4 Left onto bridge over Purisima Creek, then immediate **Right** on Purisima Creek Trail after crossing bridge.

3.5 Right on paved Higgins Purisima Road after exiting parking lot.

7.8 Left on Highway 1 at stop sign.

(To reach railroad station: **0.0 Right** on Main Street at Highway 1. **0.4 Left** on Poplar Street. **1.1 Left** on Railroad Avenue (building on right). **1.2 Left** on Grove Street. **1.6 Right** on Highway 1.)

11.0 Left on Purisima Creek Road. 11.3 Purisima town site on left.

As you ride on the trails in Purisima Creek Open Space Preserve, imagine what it must have looked like when Purisima Canyon was clear-cut. Fortunately, today we can enjoy the tranquil beauty of the lower canyon, with its 80-year-old redwood groves, fern-draped canyon walls, and burbling Purisima Creek.

In the mid- to late-1800s, dozens of logging roads were created by oxen dragging logs to nearby mills in the Santa Cruz Mountains. Purisima Creek Road is one such logging road. Rufus Hatch and George Borden began logging the canyon in the 1850s; a sawmill in the lower canyon was operated until the early 1920s. The road was used again by logging trucks in the 1960s and 1970s.

Start riding from the Purisima Creek Midpeninsula Regional Open Space District parking lot on Skyline Boulevard, 2.4 miles north of Kings Mountain Road. Take the steep Harkins Fire Trail to the bottom of Purisima Canyon, ride west to the coast on Higgins Purisima Road, turn south on Highway 1, and finish by riding up Purisima Canyon.

Early in the ride you'll skirt the upper reaches of Whittemore Gulch on a narrow trail on the way to Harkins Fire Trail. Harkins has views of the ocean and brush-covered ridges. But on a summer day the coast can be fogged in. It can be sweltering on Skyline but damp and cool in the canyon.

Leave the park on Higgins Purisima Road after crossing Purisima Creek on a wooden bridge. San Mateo County paved the road for the first time in 1987. Turn right and climb for a half-mile before descending to Highway 1. Vegetable fields line the coast. In a field on the left, look for the white-frame Johnston house, built in 1853 by James Johnston.

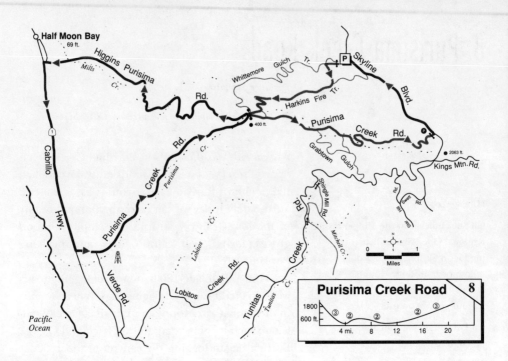

Purisima Creek Road 8

11.4 **Keep left** at Verde Road junction. 12.5 Oil well on right in field. 14.9 Gate to Purisima Creek Trail. Begin climb to Skyline. 16.3 Grabtown Gulch Trail on right. Goes to Tunitas Creek Road.

19.2 **Left** on Skyline Boulevard. 19.5 Richards Road trail on right. 19.8 Snack bar.

21.2 Return to start at parking lot.

He made his fortune as a land speculator and saloon keeper in San Francisco. Johnston and his three brothers built the first road from the bay to the coast through Pilarcitos Valley, just north of Highway 92.

Half Moon Bay is only a mile to the north and can be reached by turning right off Highway 1 onto Main Street. There's a bakery, a well-stocked general store, and a bike shop downtown. West of town you'll find the former Ocean Shore Railroad station on Railroad Avenue (see Mileage Log). The railroad was established in 1905 by land speculators who hoped to develop the coast from San Francisco to Santa Cruz. But the railroad, which reached Tunitas Creek, failed to catch on and was shut down in 1920.

From Higgins Purisima Road, ride south on Highway 1 to the junction of Purisima Creek Road. Purisima, a thriving community at the turn of the century, was located at the junction. All that remains today is a cypress grove. As you pass Verde Road, look for an oil derrick to the right on the far hill. The derrick was the first oil well in San Mateo County, yielding 40,000 barrels of oil from 1867 to 1948. Farther up the canyon, horses graze among oil wells in the front yards of ranch houses.

Return to Purisima Canyon at the parking lot, and begin climbing Purisima Creek Trail. The gradient goes from flat to steep and steeper yet. Climbing is hardest after crossing Purisima Creek at a left hairpin turn.

9 The Forest of Nisene Marks State Park

Distance: 38 miles
Terrain: Hilly
Traffic: Light to moderate for cars; bicyclists, hikers

Mileage Log

0.0 Start mileage at Summit Center Store on Summit Road, 3 miles south of Highway 17. Ride southeast on Summit Road. 0.2 Soquel–San Jose Road junction.

1.9 Right at Highland Way and stop sign. Take immediate left to continue on Highland. 4.7 Emergency water on left.

7.8 Right on Buzzard Lagoon Road at summit. Ormsby Trail on left.

8.3 Left uphill. Park entrance sign is just ahead.

8.7 Keep right at junction. Becomes Aptos Creek Fire Road. 10.0 Locked gate. Begin descent on Aptos Creek Fire Road in 1 mile. 10.9 Ridge Trail junction. Trail descends to Hihn's Mill Creek Road. Bikes permitted.

14.3 Keep left at junction. Ocean view at Sand Point Overlook. 19.0 Earthquake epicenter sign. 20.0 Aptos Creek crossing, no bridge. 20.3 Ride around locked gate at parking lot. 22.2 Aptos Creek Road.

23.2 Right on Soquel Drive at stop sign.

26.7 Right on Porter Street at traffic light. Becomes Soquel–San Jose Road. 30.0 Casalegno Store.

Every off-road rider dreams of the secluded trail in the redwoods winding endlessly downhill. Aptos Creek Fire Road in The Forest of Nisene Marks State Park comes close to the fantasy. You'll descend gradually for 13 miles on a dirt road. Ocean views, a madrone forest, and a creek crossing add to the fun.

The ride starts at Summit Center Store on Summit Road, about 3 miles southeast of Highway 17. The store was destroyed in the 1989 Loma Prieta earthquake, but was rebuilt and reopened in 1992. Summit Store is the only place you can buy food and drink until Aptos.

Ride southeast on Summit Road, which becomes Highland Way. Highland drops gently downhill as it follows a ridge overlooking the deep, wooded Soquel Canyon. After about six miles you'll ride through the upper end of Soquel Creek Canyon, following the creek on your right. In the canyon itself, there's another interesting road to explore: Hihn's Mill Road follows Soquel Creek gently downhill. It's a steep ride up to Soquel–San Jose Road. The road is named for Frederick A. Hihn, a German who arrived in Santa Cruz in 1851. He later found his fortune in the lumber business.

After crossing the headwaters of Soquel Creek, there's a short climb to the summit and your next turn. Highland Way becomes Eureka Canyon Road at the junction of Buzzard Lagoon Road on the right and Ormsby Trail on the left. Turn right onto Buzzard Lagoon Road to reach Aptos Creek Fire Road. Buzzard Lagoon Road climbs steadily through dense growths of tan oak and redwoods. Be sure to turn right and continue uphill where Buzzard Lagoon meets Aptos Creek Fire Road.

The fire road heads up Mt. Rosalia over smooth sandstone. Beyond the last gate, at 10 miles, the

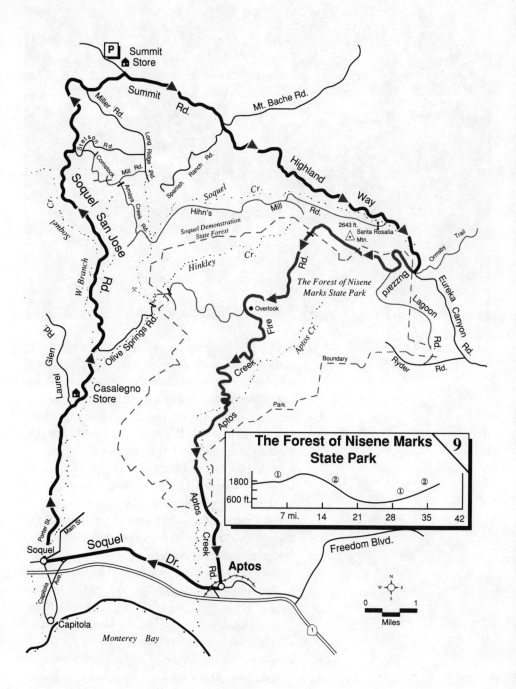

P Summit Store

Summit Rd.

Miller Rd.

Stetso Rd.

Comstock

Mill Rd.

Long Ridge Rd.

Amaya Creek Rd.

Spanish Ranch Rd.

Mt. Bache Rd.

Highland Way

Soquel Cr.

Hihn's Mill Rd.

Soquel Demonstration State Forest

Soquel Cr.

Soquel San Jose Rd.

W. Branch

Hinkley Cr.

2643 ft. Santa Rosalia Mtn.

The Forest of Nisene Marks State Park

Fire Rd.

Buzzard Lagoon Rd.

Ormsby Trail

Eureka Canyon Rd.

Overlook

Aptos Cr.

Boundary

Ryder Rd.

Laurel Glen Rd.

Creek

Olive Springs Rd.

Casalegno Store

Aptos

Park

Aptos Creek

The Forest of Nisene Marks State Park **9**

1800

600 ft.

① ② ① ②

7 mi. 14 21 28 35 42

Freedom Blvd.

Porter St.

Main St.

Soquel

Soquel Dr.

Capitola Ave.

Aptos

Rd.

N
W E
S

0 1
Miles

Capitola

Monterey Bay

1

Riders take a break at Sand Point Overlook in The Forest of Nisene Marks State Park.

37.6 Left on Summit Road at stop sign.

37.8 End ride at Summit Center Store.

road levels before descending through a forest of madrone, identified by its flaky red bark and smooth green wood. Road conditions on Aptos Creek Fire Road vary with the season, but the best riding is in the spring and early winter when the road is hardpacked. The road becomes dusty in the summer and muddy after heavy rains.

Watch for hikers, bicyclists, and equestrians. Just before the Aptos Creek crossing there's a sign marking the epicenter of the devastating 1989 Loma Prieta earthquake. Near the bottom of the canyon you'll cross Aptos Creek twice, first on a bridge and then by fording.

Note the railroad ties embedded in the road just before you cross the bridge. Aptos Canyon was logged from 1883 to 1923 by the Loma Prieta Lumber Company, which built a sawmill and town near the creek. The mill was served by a standard gauge Southern Pacific railroad 7 miles into the canyon from Aptos. All but a handful of old-growth redwoods were cut. The coastal community of Aptos grew around the logging industry, dating as far back as the 1830s. By the 1880s, two large sawmills were situated north of town and serviced by local railroads.

In 1963, Andrew Marks and Herman Agnes donated 9,600 acres of former lumber company land to the state, in memory of their mother, Nisene Marks. Today the park has more than 30 miles of hiking trails and fire roads. Cyclo-cross races have been held near the park entrance, next to Aptos Creek Fire Road.

You'll return on Soquel–San Jose Road (also called Old San Jose Highway). The road follows Soquel Creek, passing apple orchards and residential developments in the lower valley. Old San Jose Road follows the original toll road built through the canyon in 1858. Highway 17 to the north wasn't built until 1916, and didn't take its present alignment until 1940.

At the junction with Laurel Glen Road you'll pass Casalegno Store, a classic country store. *Casalegno* is Italian for wooden house, but it was also the name of the store's owner, George Casalegno.

Railroad ties can still be seen on Aptos Creek Fire Road.

The epicenter of the 1989 Loma Prieta earthquake is located near this marker on Aptos Creek Fire Road.

10 Gazos Creek Road

Distance: 28 miles
Terrain: Hilly
Traffic: Bicycles, hikers, equestrians

Mileage Log

0.0 Start mileage at the junction of Gazos Creek Road and North Escape Road about a quarter-mile north of Big Basin Redwoods State Park headquarters on Highway 236. (The park's food store rents mountain bikes.) Gazos Creek Road immediately crosses a bridge over Opal Creek. 0.1 Locked gate. 0.9 Middle Ridge Road on right; you'll return on this road. 3.0 Open gate.

6.1 Right at Sandy Point Guard Station. Whitehouse Canyon Road to left. 6.2 Johansen Fire Road. Second gate on right after passing open area. 8.1 Gate at bottom of hill. 8.3 Bridge over Gazos Creek. 9.7 Log dam artifact in Gazos Creek.

11.5 Right on Cloverdale Road. Unsigned. 12.7 Butano State Park entrance. Water available inside park, 0.3 miles from park entrance.

13.6 Right onto Butano Fire Trail at paved ramp that goes uphill 15 yards to a locked aluminum gate. Lift bike over gate. Unsigned.

16.2 Keep right at junction. 16.8 Gate, usually open. 18.7 Cross airstrip. 19.3 Butano Trail Camp on right. 19.7 Olmo Fire Road on right. 19.8 Open gate.

22.7 Right at junction onto China Grade. Locked cable across road.

For such a popular park, Big Basin Redwoods State Park has some of the most dramatic and primitive off-road riding anywhere in the Bay Area. The word has gotten out among mountain bike riders, and now the park draws riders of all abilities. On this tour you'll see burbling creeks, ancient redwoods, and experience whoop-de-doos; you'll even cross an airstrip on a lonely mountain ridge.

Road conditions change with the season. Gazos Creek Road can become a sandpit in the summer, especially after grading. A tour of the road after the winter floods of 1982–83 called for an arduous hike over downed redwoods and boulders. Nearly a mile of road was wiped off the map when Gazos Creek turned from a peaceful stream to a raging torrent.

The ride starts at park headquarters and immediately hits dirt on Gazos Creek Road, where you'll have a gentle climb followed by a brisk descent among redwoods and Douglas fir. At the bottom of the first descent, notice the hillside to the right with downed trees. The trees toppled as the earth crept down the hill. Redwoods grow to more than 200 feet, but their shallow roots make them susceptible to land movements and strong winds.

At 6 miles the Sandy Point Guard Station junction (the station burned down in the 1960s), a popular turnaround point because after a steep descent on Gazos Creek Road, the only way back is to continue the ride or return on Gazos Creek Road. The road becomes rutted and bumpy, and can be muddy in the spring. It's hard to believe that until the mid-1960s, the San Mateo County road was open to car traffic.

After the wild descent you'll reach a gate, beyond which the road is paved. The section between here and Cloverdale Road was paved in the summer of 1992. The remaining miles to

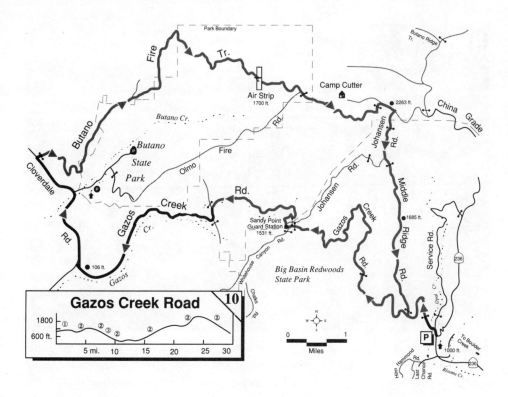

Gazos Creek Road

23.2 Right on Johansen Road.

24.1 Left on Middle Ridge Fire Road.
24.3 Locked gate. 26.1 Dooly Trail.

26.6 Left on Gazos Creek Road.

27.5 Ride ends at park headquarters.

Cloverdale Road are nothing less than heavenly as you follow the creek lined with sycamore, ash, maple, and Pacific dogwood.

In the late 1890s, Gazos Creek had a completely different complexion. It was dammed and used as a log pen for a sawmill near the road. Remnants of the redwood dam on the creek bank are visible from the road.

Turn right onto Cloverdale Road, which was paved from the ocean to Butano State Park in 1987. Your next turn is not marked, so watch carefully for Butano Fire Trail where it joins Cloverdale. There's a short, steep paved driveway leading to an aluminum gate, about 1 mile north of the Butano park entrance. The dirt road beyond the gate climbs an exposed ridge before entering a wooded canyon with impressive stands of Douglas fir. The lower parts of the canyon feature dense foliage of brambles, poison oak, and blackberries.

With one exception—noted in the mileage log— Butano Fire Trail has no road junctions. Along the way, the scenery changes from tree-covered slopes

Butano Fire Trail climbs more than 2,000 feet from the Pacific Ocean.

to granulated shale. Redwoods give way to knob-cone pines on the dry, rocky ridges. The road becomes a smooth bed of loose white shale up to an airstrip. After crossing the airstrip, you'll have a brief descent into a dark forest, followed by more, and steeper, climbing.

China Grade, altitude 2,265 feet, marks the summit. Turn right at the wire cable crossing the road. (There's a Boy Scout camp to the left.) Take China Grade, which was paved at one time, to Johansen Road, the next junction. Descend about 0.9 miles and turn left on Middle Ridge Road. It's a roller-coaster ride to Gazos Creek over sandstone and sand pits that rival anything at Spy Glass. At Gazos Creek Road turn left and return to park headquarters. Don't miss the interpretive center next to the park's concession stand.

Thanks to Andrew Hill, a San Jose artist and photographer, this area became a park in 1902. In 1900 he founded the Sempervirens Club to help create a park by raising money and lobbying to preserve old-growth redwoods. The club was revived as the Sempervirens Fund in 1968, when developers threatened to build on private land inside the park. The Los Altos–based fund has raised money to help expand the park to 19,000 acres.

11 Joseph D. Grant County Park

Distance: 8 miles
Terrain: Extremely hilly
Traffic: Bicyclists, hikers, equestrians

Mileage Log

0.0 Start ride at the entrance to Hotel Trail at green gate, located about 50 yards from the white house that serves as Joseph D. Grant County Park headquarters.

0.7 Keep right on Lower Hotel Trail. 1.5 Gate.

1.7 Circle Corral. Ride through corral to green gate. Take road to right on other side of gate. 1.8 Begin steep climb after crossing creek. 2.8 Small pond and brief respite from climb. Cañada De Pala Trail crossing.

3.5 Eagle Lake. **Keep left** of lake and begin steep descent on Digger Pine Trail.

4.5 Left on Bonhoff Trail. Begin steep climb. Right goes to Smith Creek and fire station.

5.4 Cross Mt. Hamilton Road at green gate and proceed through green gate across road. Begin Cañada De Pala Trail.

5.9 Left on Yerba Buena Trail.

8.2 End ride at parking lot for Grant Lake next to Mt. Hamilton Road.

Getting bored with the same old mountain bike rides? Looking for something that will enhance your enjoyment of flat riding? Joseph D. Grant County Park awaits. The climbs and descents will entertain even the most experienced mountain bike rider. In fact, this ride is recommended only for veteran bikers who aren't afraid of riding down hills suitable for advanced ski runs, who aren't deterred by having to walk up steep hills, and who aren't easily bullied by ornery cattle.

The ride starts innocently enough as Hotel Trail takes you through Halls Valley on a flat ranch road. Watch out for cow pies. The valley puts on an impressive wildflower display in the spring. But at the Circle Corral it's time to circle the wagons. The road climbs briskly at about a 15-percent grade and hardly lets up until Eagle Lake. The small, solitary lake offers a welcome respite from the climb.

What goes up must come down. Digger Pine Trail drops steeply to a stream where you'll pick your way through rocky sections. The road goes straight up and straight down several more times before leveling at a meadow and Bohnhoff Trail. Bohnhoff is the cliff on your left. After walking up Bohnhoff, you're greeted by a section of fairly level riding between short, steep climbs. At Mt. Hamilton Road you can see where you've been, far below. After some more climbing, you'll turn left onto Yerba Buena Trail and pick your way down to a parking lot at Grant Lake. The trail is hard to follow in places because it becomes a cattle trail next to Mt. Hamilton Road. There's one particularly steep, loose spot to watch for as you approach Mt. Hamilton Road and the fence.

The ride may be only 8 miles, but it feels like 50. Helmets are required to ride in the Santa Clara

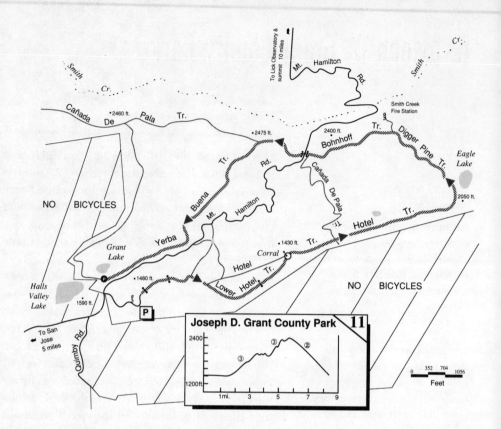

County park. You should also check in at park headquarters, the white ranch house on your left at the start of Hotel Trail.

12 Henry W. Coe State Park

Distance: 16 miles
Terrain: Extremely hilly
Traffic: Equestrians, hikers, bicyclists

Mileage Log

0.0 To reach Henry W. Coe State Park, take Highway 101 south to the Dunne Avenue exit in Morgan Hill. Go left (east) and drive up a narrow, curvy road 13 miles to the park entrance. There's a $5 parking fee. Start mileage at Pacheco Route, from the yellow gate across the headquarters parking lot.

0.4 Left at Northern Heights Route to monument, uphill. 0.9 Monument on right. 1.0 Begin descent to Frog Lake. (Take trail at mile 1.6 to visit lake; otherwise stay left on road.) 1.9 Begin climb.

2.8 Right on Middle Ridge Trail. View point straight ahead. 3.1 Frog Lake junction on right. 4.3 Fish Trail junction on right. 5.0 Begin steep descent. 6.4 Middle Fork Coyote Creek.

6.6 Left on Pacheco Route. 7.9 Trailhead on right. You'll return here. 8.1 Los Cruzeros camp junction on right.

9.1 Keep left at junction. Begin climb on Northern Heights Route.

9.9 Left at clearing. Go 20 feet and turn left again on Jackass Trail. Right at trail marker, uphill. 10.1 Begin descent.

If you're an avid snow skier, you've probably seen one of those B movies with the daredevil skiers doing hair-raising stunts. Maybe someday they'll make a mountain bike movie featuring wild and crazy riding. Its producer would find Henry W. Coe State Park a suitable location. The park's remote trails and roads test the best riders' abilities. Don't ride here unless you know how to handle a bike, you're a strong rider, and you're safety conscious. In the event of an accident, it could be many hours before a rescue, as the park is enormous. Our second largest state park, 20 miles southeast of San Jose, encompasses nearly 100 square miles.

More than 200 miles of ranch roads and trails touch every section of the park, although mountain bikes are prohibited in the Orestimba Wilderness Area. Nearly every road is either straight up or straight down. But in the spring you can take a break during the ride and enjoy the park's spectacular wildflower display. In the fall you'll have autumn colors and cool, crisp air to breathe. Weather can be severe—brutally hot and freezing cold. Water is available at park headquarters only.

The route makes a figure-eight loop that includes two sections of single-track. The rest of the ride takes dirt roads. Always expect to encounter other trail users around the next turn. Note that Middle Ridge Trail is closed to mountain bikes for 48 hours after significant rains. Check with the ranger before riding.

Start at a yellow gate across the road from park headquarters. Take Pacheco Route for 0.4 miles and turn left, uphill. Northern Heights Route rises steeply across an exposed ridge. Look for a granite

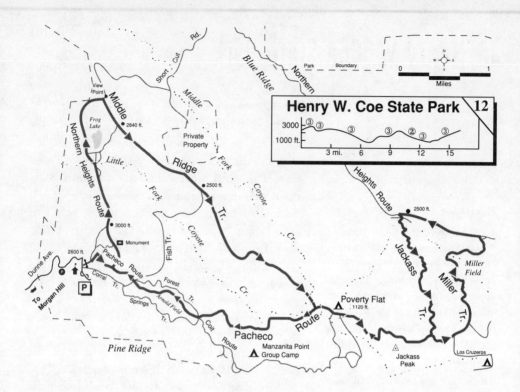

11.3 **Right** back onto Pacheco Route.

12.7 Begin climb.

14.4 **Keep right.** Manzanita Point junction on left.

16.0 End ride at park headquarters.

monument dedicated to Henry Coe at the summit among pine trees.

Descend for about a mile to Frog Lake. The road circles the small lake, which is out of sight below you. There's a gradual climb to the Deerhorn Viewpoint and Middle Ridge Trail. Middle Ridge begins just before the overlook on the right, at the "Frog Lake" marker.

The overlook reveals a breathtaking view of Blue Ridge and the perilously steep Short Cut Road. After taking in the view, turn around and pick up Middle Ridge Trail. The trail rolls along for the next 2 miles before dropping steeply to the Middle Fork of Coyote Creek. Keep left at the two junctions. The rocky creek is fun to ford when water is running in the spring. Ride a short distance to Pacheco Route and turn left. Continue east up Jackass Peak from Poverty Flat backpack camp; there's a steep climb of less than a mile. On the other side, at Miller Field, you'll have a couple of steep hills. Keep left at the three major junctions.

After the third junction, you'll climb Northern Heights Route for about a mile.

To find the single-track trail, watch the left side of the road and check your cyclometer (see Mileage Log). After riding through oak trees on a steep section, you'll come to a flat spot with a small clearing on the left. Go west about 20 feet off the road and pick up Jackass Trail running north-south. Go left on the trail, and begin climbing through some oak trees. In about 50 yards you'll come to a trail post. Turn right onto the trail and continue climbing. Soon you'll reach a clearing with a splendid view of the park to the south and west. The trail winds down the hill through mesquite and open meadows, bringing you back to Miller Field and the ranch road.

Return to headquarters by Pacheco Route. The climb from Poverty Flat has two steep sections early on. Then the road levels and climbs again less steeply to Arnold Field.

The park is named for Henry Coe, whose sons and daughters carried on the tradition of raising cattle at nearby Pine Ridge Ranch. Sada Coe, Henry's daughter, donated the ranch to Santa Clara County in 1953. Over the years, several more ranches were added to the park. Cattle ranching continues at several private inholdings. Don't be surprised by the occasional rancher's truck.

Overnight campgrounds near park headquarters are available, or you can ride into the park to camp at designated sites. Camping reservations are first come, first served.

Poison oak thrives on the park's many steep slopes and canyons. Know what it looks like and avoid it. For more information, write Henry W. Coe State Park, P.O. Box 846, Morgan Hill, CA 95037. Phone (408) 779-2728.

13 Old Haul Road

Distance: 18 miles
Terrain: Gentle grades on Old Haul Road; otherwise hilly
Traffic: Light; bicycles, hikers, equestrians

Mileage Log

0.0 Start mileage at Old Haul Road Trailhead on Wurr Road, next to Memorial County Park. The trailhead is 0.3 miles south of Pescadero Road and about a half-mile north of the Memorial Park entrance. Ride toward Pescadero Road.

0.3 Right on Pescadero Road at stop sign. 3.0 Haskins Hill summit. 3.8 Entrance to Sam McDonald County Park.

4.3 Right on Alpine Road. 5.6 Heritage Grove old-growth redwoods on right. 6.0 Begin Alpine Road ascent.

8.0 Stay left at Pomponio Road junction and honor camp entrance.

8.4 Right on Portola Park Road at stop sign. Begin descent. 10.6 Portola State Park boundary. 11.8 Park headquarters and interpretive center. Restrooms and water. 12.0 Ride around gate on "Service Area" road.

12.6 Right on narrow trail immediately after crossing bridge over Pescadero Creek. Walk bike. 12.7 Iverson cabin. Ride up steep road.

12.8 Right on Old Haul Road at gate.

13.9 Stay left at Bridge Trail junction.

Deep in the redwoods in San Mateo County there's a popular recreation path built on a railroad right-of-way with gradual ups and downs. Of course, you won't see a train today, only hikers, bicyclists, and equestrians. A 42-ton oil-burning Shay locomotive ran from 1921 to 1951, hauling logs to the Santa Cruz Lumber Company mill near Waterman Gap. Log trucks did the work of the train until 1972, when the mill was shut down.

The lumber company sold half its forested lands to public agencies in 1970, contributing to the newly formed Pescadero Creek County Park in San Mateo County. At the county park's eastern boundary is Portola State Park, which was founded in 1945. The county park's 7,000 acres include many miles of hiking trails, some of them connecting with Portola State Park's 2,400 acres.

In the spring, yellow-flowered Western broom creates an enchanting corridor on the Old Haul Road. There's a scenic view around every bend. Numerous brooks trickle down Butano Ridge and feed into the densely wooded Pescadero Creek. During the winter of 1982–83, these peaceful streams raged out of control, uprooting redwoods and destroying the road. In 1984, work crews from the sheriff's honor farm, located in the park, pitched in to repair the road and clear brush. Today the road is hardpacked, with numerous graveled sections, making it ridable year-round. Trail signs mark every junction.

Start your ride next to Memorial Park, which has picnic grounds, camping facilities, restrooms, water fountains, and a swimming area. You'll take Pescadero and Alpine roads, returning through Portola State Park and the Old Haul Road. For a much easier ride, take the Old Haul Road out and back.

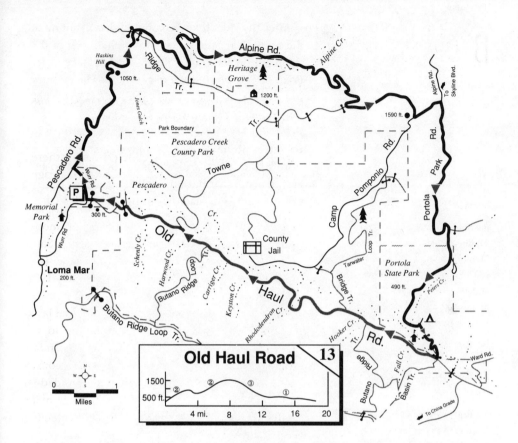

Old Haul Road 13

16.7 Left at junction. Crucial inter-section. Towne Trail goes straight. No bikes allowed.

17.6 Continue straight and ride around gate.

17.7 Stay right at junction.

18.1 Ride ends at Wurr Road and locked gate.

Pescadero Road has a 2-mile climb over Haskins Hill, followed by a 1-mile descent to Alpine Road. You'll have 4 miles of uphill before you begin a fast descent to Portola State Park. Inside the park, ride past the campgrounds and pick up the service road. Cross Pescadero Creek on a wooden bridge, and walk your bike a short distance on a narrow trail, which leads to the rickety Iverson cabin. Christian Iverson, a Scandinavian immigrant who worked as a Pony Express rider and armed guard, built the cabin in the 1860s. The building has col-lapsed and been resurrected several times. Continue on the paved road, which crosses Pescadero Creek and goes up to the Old Haul Road. Turn right at the gate.

Take Bridge Trail if you want to see Pescadero Creek. A Bailey-type bridge spans the creek.

After the ride, there's food and drink waiting at the Loma Mar Store, a mile and a half west of the trailhead on Pescadero Road. You can take Wurr Road or Pescadero Road to get there. The country store has a fireplace, pool table, and TV. Owner Roger Siebecker runs the business seven days a week and also serves as the town postmaster and volunteer fireman. You'll enjoy relaxing on the store's front patio and watching the world go by. For more information, call Pescadero Creek County Park, San Mateo County, (415) 363-4020.

14 Skyline to the Sea Trail

Distance: 11 miles
Terrain: Gentle hills
Traffic: Bicyclists, hikers, equestrians

Mileage Log

0.0 Start riding from Waddell Beach on Highway 1, about 10 miles north of Santa Cruz. Find a brown gate with a sign marking the Skyline to the Sea Trail.

0.3 Left at park office and parking lot for horse trailers. Ride around two gates. Watch for signs indicating Skyline to the Sea Trail. Bicyclists must stay on the dirt road at all times.

0.6 Keep left at junction. 3.1 Ford creek or take bridge on right. Old mill site. 5.2 Henry Creek Trail.

5.6 Trail ends for bicycling. Turn around and return same way.

10.8 Keep right. Don't go down the road to the left.

11.3 Ride ends at Highway 1.

In a remote section of the Santa Cruz Mountains you'll find one of nature's most unusual displays—a waterfall in the redwoods. Berry Creek Falls, centrally located in Big Basin Redwoods State Park, is well worth the hike, but you can see it much more easily by bike. Take Skyline to the Sea Trail, which will bring you within a short distance of the falls. The dirt road begins at the Pacific Ocean and extends inland more than 5 miles as it follows Waddell Creek. The smooth, well-maintained road has an easy grade through the redwoods. The best time to visit is in the spring, although the waterfall flows year-round.

No doubt local Indians frequented the lush Waddell Creek canyon. Spaniards who foraged in the canyon in the 1760s called it Cañada de la Salud, or Canyon of Health. They and later settlers had to contend with grizzly bears. William Waddell, for whom the creek is named, was killed by a grizzly bear in the canyon in 1875. In 1862, Waddell had built a sawmill where the east and west forks of the creek join, a few miles inland from the ocean. The mill site is marked by a small park sign.

The road takes you to within a quarter-mile of the waterfall. You must park your bike and walk the rest of the way on a narrow trail on which bikes are not permitted.

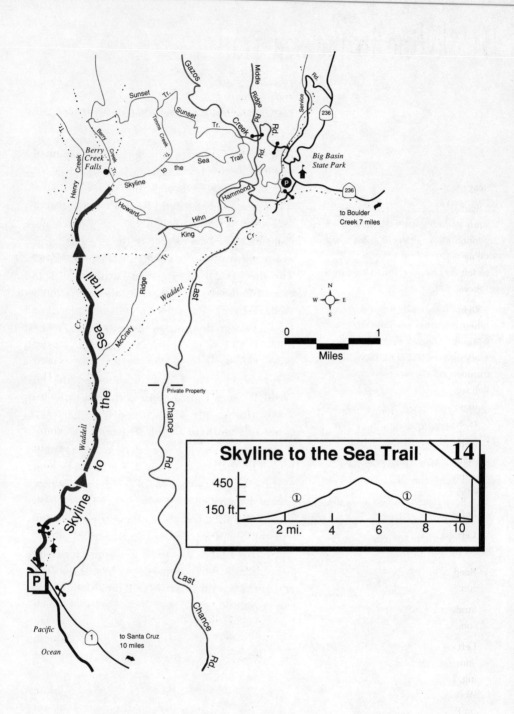

Sunset Tr.

Gazos Creek

Sunset Tr.

Middle Ridge Rd.

Service Rd.

236

Berry Creek Falls

Berry Creek Tr.

Timms Creek Tr.

to the Sea Trail

Henry Creek Tr.

Skyline

Howard

Hammond

Big Basin State Park

P

236

to Boulder Creek 7 miles

Hihn

King

Tr.

Cr.

Waddell

Last

McCrary

Ridge

Chance

Rd.

Private Property

Pacific

Ocean

1

to Santa Cruz 10 miles

Last Chance Rd.

Waddell

Cr.

Sea

Trail

the

to

Skyline

P

N
W   E
S

0   1

Miles

Skyline to the Sea Trail 14

450
150 ft.

①   ①

2 mi.   4   6   8   10

15 Stevens Canyon

Distance: 21 miles
Terrain: Hilly
Traffic: Light for cars; bicyclists, hikers, equestrians

Stevens Canyon has the distinction of being one of the nearest and most accessible trail rides for cyclists living on the southern end of the Peninsula. The recreation trail extends the length of the canyon, directly over the San Andreas Fault. The canyon trail has a long history. In the late 1800s it was a "skid road" for hauling redwood logs by ox. More recently, the road was used by farmers and ranchers who had orchards on the surrounding ridges.

The ride starts in Stevens Creek County Park, a few miles west of Cupertino at the site of an old ranch and Villa Maria winery. The winery was used by Santa Clara University from 1872 to 1944. The first settler in the area, Captain Elisha Stephens, settled here in 1850. Park headquarters, down the hill from the parking lot, houses a small museum.

After riding past Stevens Creek Reservoir—an earthen dam built in 1936—you'll begin a long climb on Montebello Road, which has an average grade of 7–8 percent. The first mile is the steepest, with one short pitch as steep as 15 percent. On the way up you'll pass Picchetti Winery and Ridge Winery. The Picchetti property is leased from the Midpeninsula Regional Open Space District (MROSD) by Sunrise Winery in Boulder Creek. MROSD, a public land agency, maintains the ranch and winery, built in the 1870s. The historic site includes a wine cellar and old wine equipment. Wine tastings are held Friday, Saturday, and Sunday, 11:00 A.M. to 3:00 P.M.

Ridge Winery, located in an old ranch house overlooking Santa Clara Valley high up on Montebello Ridge, is open Saturdays for wine tasting. The prestigious winery was established in the late 1800s. It shut down for a time but was revived

Mileage Log

0.0 Start mileage at Stevens Creek County Park from first signed parking lot on Stevens Canyon Road. Ride up steep hill for 25 yards and turn left on Stevens Canyon Road. 0.7 Stevens Creek Dam.

1.2 Right on Montebello Road. 1.7 Picchetti Ranch and Sunrise Winery. 2.6 Jimsomare vineyard. 5.6 Ridge Winery on left. 6.4 Locked gate. Continue north on paved road, which soon turns to dirt. 8.0 Black Mountain summit with microwave towers. 8.2 Gate.

8.5 Keep right at junction. If you want water from a spigot at the backpack camp, go left at junction for 0.1 miles. 9.5 Locked Gate.

10.0 Left on Page Mill Road at gate.

10.5 Left at entrance to signed Stevens Canyon Trail.

11.7 Keep right at Indian Creek Trail junction.

13.6 Straight at Grizzly Flat Trail junction.

14.0 Left up trail. Note Saratoga Gap Trail junction on right in circular clearing. 14.4 Ford Stevens Creek. 14.7 Wooden barrier. 14.8 Stevens Canyon Road begins. 15.1 Cross Stevens Creek pouring over road. 17.2 Redwood Gulch Road intersection.

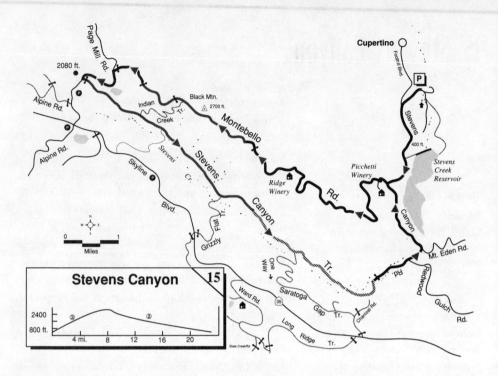

Stevens Canyon 15

18.8 Left at stop sign. Mt. Eden Road on right.

21.4 End of ride at parking lot.

in 1962 by two Palo Alto residents. They sold the winery in 1987.

It's another mile from Ridge Winery to a locked gate you can walk your bike around. The pavement ends shortly after the gate. The final climb to Black Mountain summit goes over a ridge with views of the Pacific and San Francisco Bay. If you want to cut the ride short, you can descend Indian Creek Trail to Stevens Canyon. To do so, take the first left on a ranch road as you descend from the top of Black Mountain. You'll find the trailhead sign about 0.3 miles down the road next to a ranch house. Indian Creek Trail is a wide, steep road.

For the measured ride, continue north to Page Mill Road and turn left. Stevens Trail joins Page Mill on the left at a dip in the road. You'll descend 1,200 feet on the steep trail in the next 5 miles. In the dry season, the terrain changes from meadows of golden wild oats to oaks, buckeye, tan oak, and finally redwoods and Douglas fir deep in the damp, dark canyon.

Telltale signs of sinkholes and distorted earth can be seen 200 yards after taking Stevens Canyon

Trail at Page Mill Road. On the left, in a thicket of willows, there's a sag pond that's choked with lilies.

Deep in the canyon, you'll come to a circular clearing where there's a one-way trail sign for Saratoga Gap on the right. You'll take the narrow trail on the left, going uphill. Watch out for poison oak. After a short, steep descent, you'll ford Stevens Creek and cross a landslide. Cross Stevens Creek once again (it spills over the paved road), and you're back on pavement. It's mostly downhill to Stevens Creek Reservoir. Stevens Canyon can be enjoyed year-round, but it's especially nice on hot days or in the fall when the leaves are turning. Helmets are required in Upper Stevens Canyon Park.

Stevens Canyon Trail descends steeply into a cool, damp redwood forest.

II. Road Rides

16 Napa Valley

Distance: 16 or 53 miles
Terrain: Flat or hilly
Traffic: Light to heavy

Mileage Log

RIDE 1: VALLEY TOUR

0.0 Start mileage at intersection of Pope Street and Highway 29 and ride east on Pope. Parking available at nearby high school.

0.8 Right on Silverado Trail at stop sign after crossing stone bridge over Napa River. 5.3 ZD Winery on right.

7.3 Right on Oakville Cross Road.

9.8 Right on Highway 29 at stop sign. 11.8 BV Winery on right. Beware of train tracks on Highway 29. 12.2 Beware of train tracks. 14.4 Heitz Cellars winery on right. 14.5 Louis Martini winery on right. 14.8 Christian Brothers winery on right.

15.6 End ride at start.

RIDE 2: MOUNTAIN TOUR

0.0 Start mileage at corner of Deer Park Road and Highway 29. Parking available in St. Helena. Ride north on Highway 29 to Calistoga. 1.7 Old Bale Grist Mill State Park. 3.4 Bothe Napa Valley State Park.

6.8 Right on Lincoln Avenue at stop sign (Highway 29) to downtown Calistoga.

7.8 Keep left at Silverado Trail junction.

Napa Valley is known for its vineyards and wineries, but it also has some of the most interesting bike riding in Northern California. Fall may be the best season for touring the vineyards, as grape leaves turn color, the harvest is over, and the tourists have left. Cool mornings give way to warm, sunny afternoons. On weekends colorful hot-air balloons drift across clear blue skies, and white gliders soar on updrafts along The Palisades overlooking the town of Calistoga.

One of the best places to start a ride in Napa Valley is the town of St. Helena, centrally located for both bicycling and wine tasting. The short, flat ride described here loops through the valley, passing more than 20 wineries—Sutter Home, Louis Martini, Robert Mondavi, Christian Brothers, and others.

Start early to avoid the heat and traffic on Highway 29, the busiest road in the valley. Most wineries have tastings from 10:00 A.M. to 4:00 P.M. Train tracks crossing Highway 29 at two locations are probably the worst hazard you'll encounter. Because they cross the road diagonally, slow down and take them at right angles. To be perfectly safe, you can always dismount and walk across. The two-lane Silverado Trail carries much less traffic than Highway 29. It also offers better views because it overlooks the valley in many places.

The long, hilly ride leaves the vineyards behind in pursuit of rural scenery and spectacular views of the valley. Along the way, you'll have numerous opportunities to stop and see interesting landmarks. Don't miss the Bale Grist Mill. The giant wooden waterwheel is 36 feet in diameter and weighs 5.5 tons. It was built in 1846 by Dr. Edward Bale. The flour mill closed in 1905; in 1974 the mill

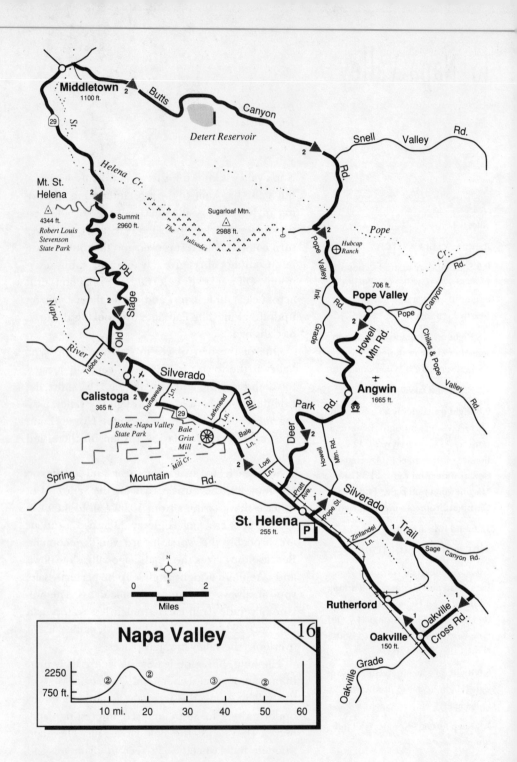

Middletown
1100 ft.

Butts

Canyon

Detert Reservoir

Snell Valley Rd.

29

St.

Helena Cr.

Mt. St. Helena

4344 ft.
Robert Louis Stevenson State Park

• Summit 2960 ft.

The Palisades

Sugarloaf Mtn.

2988 ft.

Pope

Pope Valley Rd.

Hubcap Ranch

Cr.

Rd.

706 ft.

Pope Valley

Napa

River

Old Stage Rd.

Tubbs Ln.

Silverado

Trail

Ink Grade Rd.

Pope

Howell Mtn Rd.

Chiles & Pope Valley Rd.

Duhawe Ln.

Calistoga 2
365 ft.

29

Bothe -Napa Valley State Park

Bale Grist Mill

Larkmead Ln.

Bale Ln.

Mill Cr.

Lodi Ln.

Deer Park Rd.

Howell Mtn. Rd.

Angwin
1665 ft.

Spring Mountain Rd.

2

Pratt Ave.

1

Silverado

Trail

St. Helena
255 ft.

P

Pope St.

Zinfandel Ln.

1

Sage Canyon Rd.

Rutherford

1

Oakville Cross Rd.

Oakville
150 ft.

Oakville Grade

N
W · E
S

0   2
Miles

Napa Valley

16

2250

750 ft.

② ②   ③   ②

10 mi.   20   30   40   50   60

9.3 Right on Old Stage Road, also called Lawley Road. Begin steep 4.7-mile climb in 0.9 miles.

12.6 Right on Highway 29 at stop sign, continuing climb. 14.6 Summit. Robert Louis Stevenson State Park on left, and hiking trail to Mt. St. Helena summit. 15.2 Unpaved service road to Mt. St. Helena summit, open to bicycles. 18.1 Lake County. 23.8 Downtown Middletown. Food and drink.

24.4 Right on Butts Canyon Road at cemetery. 29.0 Oat Hill Road junction on right. 29.7 Detert Reservoir. 35.5 Snell Valley Road junction on left. Butts Canyon Road becomes Pope Valley Road. Begin 1.1-mile climb. 36.6 Summit. Begin 1.3-mile descent to Pope Valley. 38.4 Bridge over Pope Creek. 40.6 Hubcap Ranch.

42.9 Right on Howell Mountain Road in Pope Valley at stop sign. Begin steep 2.3-mile climb. 45.2 Summit. 46.7 Straight at College Avenue junction. 47.0 Town of Angwin. 48.9 Howell Mountain Road changes name to Deer Park Road at four-way intersection. 52.8 Continue straight at stop sign for Silverado Trail.

53.5 Ride ends at start.

site became a state historic park, and restoration began in 1980.

On the way up Highway 29 you'll have impressive views of Napa Valley, the rocky red cliffs of The Palisades, and Sugarloaf Mountain. Instead of taking Highway 29 all the way, try Old Stage Road (or Lawley Road). The narrow, bumpy road was built by John Lawley in 1874 as a toll road. Lawley, an early entrepreneur in Napa Valley, had good business sense when he built the road. It became the best route to Mt. St. Helena, which at the time was one giant mine shaft, with mining towns like Silverado clinging to its slopes.

When the railroad reached Calistoga in 1868, Lawley realized that a properly graded road would speed deliveries to the mines. The alternate route, up Oat Hill Road, between Calistoga and Middletown, was even steeper than the route Lawley built. Three years after completing the road, Lawley built the Toll House, a family residence, inn, and horse stable at the road's summit. The original house burned in 1883. A second house built at the same site burned in 1951. In 1923 the state purchased the toll road and built Highway 29, although the upper highway still follows Lawley Road.

Two well-known figures associated with Mt. St. Helena were the writer Robert Louis Stevenson and the robber Black Bart. Stevenson wrote *Treasure Island, The Strange Case of Dr. Jekyll and Mr. Hyde,* and *Kidnapped.* In 1880 he lived on the mountain with his bride. Their residence is gone, but you can still visit the site in Robert Louis Stevenson Park by hiking in 1 mile from the Highway 29 summit parking lot.

Charles Boles, alias Black Bart, also frequented the hills above Calistoga, robbing—with an unloaded gun—Wells Fargo stagecoaches traveling the toll road. His eight-year crime spree lasted until 1883. He spent his remaining years in San Quentin prison.

You can't miss Hubcap Ranch on Pope Valley Road. The ranch has been declared a state historic landmark. Litto Diamonte, an Italian immigrant, moved to the valley to farm in the early 1900s. His hubcap collection, which started as a joke, grew into thousands, until hubcaps covered the house and barn and lined the fences. Diamonte died in 1983, but his legacy shines on.

Pope Valley has a store where you can get food and drink before the final steep climb. The store is closed on Saturdays, however, as are all stores in the town of Angwin, built by the Seventh-day Adventists. Near the end of the ride you'll get a chance to test your gears on Howell Mountain Road leading to Angwin. The 2-mile ascent has a grade of 9–13 percent.

17 Russian River

Distance: 61 miles
Terrain: Hilly
Traffic: Light to moderate

Mileage Log

0.0 Start mileage in downtown Guerneville at the intersection of Highway 116 and Mill Street. Ride west toward the ocean on Highway 116. 0.6 Old Cazadero Road.

6.6 Right on Austin Creek Road.

10.1 Left onto bridge over Austin Creek.

10.2 Right on Cazadero Highway. 12.9 Town of Cazadero. One main store open daily.

13.3 Left at junction with King Ridge Road. Begin steep climb. 18.5 Summit. Begin 2.3-mile descent and level section.

22.4 Left on Meyers Grade at stop sign. Summit. 25.5 Begin descent to Highway 1.

27.3 Left on Highway 1 at stop sign. 31.7 Town of Jenner. Restrooms and food at mile 32.5. Restrooms next to Russian River at interpretive center. 33.6 Highway 116. Cross Russian River.

40.2 Left on Coleman Valley Road. Watch for row of tall cypress. 41.7 Top of steep part of climb. Gradual ascent to mile 45.5. 46.5 Coleman Valley. 48.1 Begin climb out of valley. 48.8 Summit. Begin 1.5-mile descent.

Riding on Sonoma County back roads gives the cyclist a new appreciation for Northern California. Between quiet rural communities you'll see redwoods, the rocky Pacific shoreline, and sheep grazing in picturesque meadows.

Start the ride in the town of Guerneville, on the banks of the Russian River. The former sawmill town was founded in 1865. The sawmill turned out railroad ties for the transcontinental railroad. In its early years, Guerneville was called Stumptown for the many tree stumps left by loggers. Later, the town was renamed Guerneville after George Guerne, an early mill owner.

Ride west toward the coast on Highway 116. The two-lane road sees heavy use in the summer, but it has wide shoulders in most sections. The road follows the right-of-way of a former standard-gauge railroad to Monte Rio and then an old wagon road to Cazadero Highway.

Old Cazadero Road is on your right in a half-mile, but continue straight, unless you're interested in some dirt-road riding to get to Cazadero. This paved road climbs steeply, then turns to dirt for the descent to East Austin Creek. Because there isn't a bridge across the creek, take this route only in the summer. For the measured route, turn right on Austin Creek Road. The old, narrow road to Cazadero has little traffic.

The narrow-gauge North Pacific Coast Railroad ran along Austin Creek at the turn of the century. Trains hauled logs to Duncans Mills on the Russian River, and took passengers on to Sausalito.

Follow the wide, shallow Austin Creek for several miles before crossing a bridge to pick up Cazadero Highway, a wide, smooth road, first paved in 1960. Cazadero, formerly a bustling logging town nestled

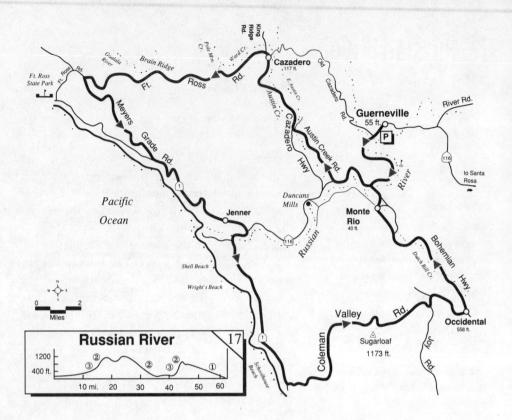

Russian River 17

50.3 **Left** at stop sign in town of Occidental onto Bohemian Highway. Road becomes Main Street a half-mile from Monte Rio.

56.7 **Left** at stop sign in town of Monte Rio onto bridge over Russian River.

56.9 **Right** at junction. Begin Highway 116 after stop sign.

60.9 End of ride in Guerneville.

in a canyon, is a wide spot in the road today. It has two churches, a tennis court, a few stores, and the Cazadero Inn.

Cazadero Highway becomes Fort Ross Road heading north out of town. The road wasn't paved until around 1963 and was called Stefani Road. Keep left at the King Ridge Road junction. King Ridge Road was the route taken by a stage of the Coors Classic bicycle race. The road gets hilly here, climbing steeply from 177 feet to more than 1,400 feet.

With almost no traffic to interrupt your solitude, you can take your time and enjoy the rolling hills among redwoods and Douglas fir, with views of a deep canyon to the north.

From Fort Ross Road, turn left on Meyers Grade. In 1811 it was a trail used by Russians traveling between Bodega Bay and Ft. Ross. On a day without coastal fog you can see the Pacific from amidst wildflower meadows, redwoods, and conifers. The rugged coast and pounding surf form an inspiring backdrop to begin a breathtaking winding descent to Highway 1.

On the Coast Highway you will pass Sonoma Coast State Beach. Nearby, at the mouth of the Russian River, seals often congregate. Look for them piled up like driftwood. A short distance farther, the village of Jenner makes a good food stop. There's an interpretive center with a small pier and restrooms at the bottom of the hill.

Continue south for 9 miles on Highway 1 to Coleman Valley Road, where you'll turn left. A row of cypress lining the road marks the turnoff. Begin climbing a steep hill of less than a mile to an exposed ridge with numerous rock outcroppings. In the spring wild iris line the road. Traffic is light on the narrow, bumpy road except on warm Sundays in the spring.

In the wooded Coleman Valley there's an old ranch with a few barns and Coleman Valley School, dating back to the 1870s. From the valley you'll have a short climb and then a descent to the town

Small islands called sea stacks dot the coast near Highway 1 and Meyers Grade.

of Occidental, best known for its Italian restaurants and bed-and-breakfast inns.

Complete the loop by returning on Bohemian Highway, a long gradual downhill through the redwoods along Dutch Bill Creek. Ride through the town of Monte Rio, cross the Russian River on a narrow bridge (there's a sidewalk you can ride on), and then turn right to return to Guerneville on Highway 116.

Spring and fall are the best seasons for riding here, although it can be pleasant in the winter or invitingly cool along the coast on hot summer days. An offshore breeze picks up at midmorning and generally blows from the north along the coast.

18 Muir Woods

Distance: 27 miles
Terrain: Two major climbs
Traffic: Light to heavy

Mileage Log

0.0 Start mileage at the parking area under the Richardson Bay Bridge in Marin City, right off Pohono Street. Ride north on a paved recreation path. 0.1 Cross bridge over Coyote Creek.

0.5 Left, leaving path at crosswalk, and then immediate right on Miller Avenue bike lane.

2.5 Left where Miller forks in front of the bookstore. Then turn right in 15 yards at a stop sign, continuing on Miller Avenue a short distance to Throckmorton Avenue. Turn left at the Throckmorton Avenue stop sign.

2.8 Left on Cascade Avenue into Old Mill Park. Keep right at the next junction.

3.1 Left on Marion Avenue, uphill on a concrete road.

4.1 Right on Edgewood Avenue at stop sign. 4.5 Keep left on Sequoia Valley Road.

5.1 Right on Panoramic Highway at stop sign.

8.7 Left at Pan Toll park headquarters, staying on Panoramic Highway to Highway 1.

13.3 Left on Highway 1 at stop sign.

19.2 Left on Muir Woods Road. 21.7 Muir Woods National Monument. Bicycles not allowed in park. Water

Marin County's stately redwoods have attracted tourists by the millions for decades. On this ride you'll visit the world-renowned Muir Woods National Monument and the rest of the best that Marin County offers.

The ride starts in Marin City at Richardson Bay and goes north through downtown Mill Valley. The town was settled by loggers in the 1840s, who found work at a sawmill on Old Mill Creek. By 1900 the logging industry had slowed and tourism took over. Mill Valley quickly became a playground for San Francisco's rich and famous. They delighted in riding the "Crookedest Railroad in the World" to the summit of Mt. Tamalpais. The woodsy town experienced another growth spurt in 1906 when refugees from the San Francisco earthquake and fire settled here. Today, the town at the base of Mt. Tamalpais has an eclectic population of writers, entertainers, and artists.

You'll parallel the former right-of-way of the North Pacific Coast Railroad on Miller Avenue. The train depot, built in 1925, is located in Lytton Square; it's now a bookstore and coffee shop.

Leaving downtown Mill Valley, you'll pass the remnants of John Reed's sawmill in Old Mill Park. Continue northwest through the park to the winding, narrow Marion Avenue. The concrete road climbs steadily past houses clinging to steeply wooded slopes. Turn right onto Edgewood Avenue, and stay left at the Sequoia Valley Road junction.

At Panoramic Highway turn right and continue climbing on the two-lane road to the high point of the ride at 1,500 feet. On hot days, the road is crowded with traffic going to Stinson Beach. Now that the climbing is over, you can have some fun riding down to Shoreline Highway, where you'll turn left.

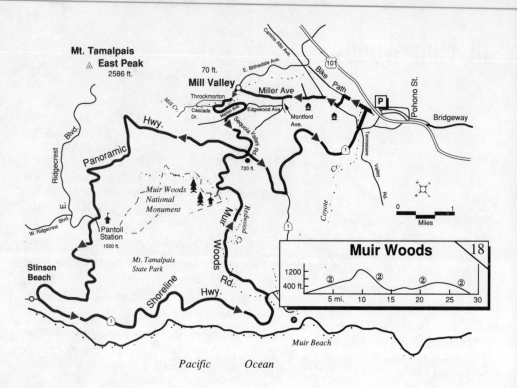

Muir Woods 18

fountains and restrooms found in parking area.

23.4 Right on Panoramic Highway at stop sign. Summit.

24.3 Left on Highway 1 at stop sign, continuing descent to bay.

26.8 Right at traffic light, staying on Highway 1. Ride about 200 yards, cross bridge and turn right on Tennessee Valley Road. Ride through gravel parking area on your right and walk or ride under bridge on a narrow path. Continue straight and pick up a paved recreation path beyond the bridge. If the path is blocked by high tide, stay on Highway 1 and return to start by riding under Richardson Bay Bridge.

Shoreline Highway between Stinson Beach and Muir Beach Overlook follows the rocky Pacific shoreline's towering cliffs before turning inland. The two-lane road has no shoulders. The road was closed for extensive repairs in 1990–91.

Turn left onto the quiet Muir Woods Road and ride up the wooded Frank Valley along Redwood Creek. The final climb starts at the entrance to Muir Woods National Monument.

Marin County's only remaining old-growth redwoods survived the ax thanks to William Kent. Kent's land faced condemnation by a water company intent on building a reservoir. Eventually the legislator learned about a little-known law that made valuable parcels into a national monument. Previous efforts to give the land to the government or have it declared a state park had failed.

27.2 Right at path junction.

27.4 Finish at parking area under bridge.

In 1908, 295 acres were presented to the U.S. government and accepted by President Teddy Roosevelt. Kent asked that the monument be named after John Muir, who campaigned to make Yosemite Valley a national park.

The descent on Highway 1 begins at the Panoramic Highway junction. Follow a recreation path back to the parking area under Highway 101, as described in the Mileage Log.

People flock to Stinson Beach on warm days.

19 Point Reyes

Distance: 54 miles
Terrain: One long climb, several short climbs
Traffic: Light to heavy

Mileage Log

0.0 Start mileage in Fairfax at the parking lot between Sir Francis Drake Boulevard and Broadway, near the junction with Fairfax Bolinas Road. Ride south on Bolinas Avenue (name changes to Fairfax Bolinas Road). 2.5 Meadow Club Golf Course. 3.7 Summit. 8.0 Cross Alpine Dam.

10.3 Right at summit and stop sign for West Ridgecrest Boulevard junction. Fairfax Bolinas Road continues to right.

14.6 Right on Highway 1 at stop sign. 15.2 Dogtown. 23.7 Olema.

23.8 Left on Bear Valley Road.

24.7 Left to Point Reyes National Seashore Park Headquarters. Return to Bear Valley Road and turn left.

26.7 Left on Sir Francis Drake Boulevard at stop sign. 27.2 Inverness Park.

29.8 Inverness. Return on Sir Francis Drake Boulevard to Highway 1, keeping left at the Bear Valley Road junction.

33.4 Left on Highway 1 at stop sign. 34.0 Ride through Point Reyes Station on Highway 1.

34.4 Right on Point Reyes–Petaluma Road.

Could it be that Marin County has one of the highest concentrations of bicyclists anywhere in the United States? They're everywhere to be seen on weekends. On the ride to Point Reyes National Seashore, you'll understand why Marin County is so popular. It's one giant park—federal, state, county, city, and public water district. Without protection, Marin County would certainly not be the rural enclave it is today.

Fairfax, last in a string of towns on Sir Francis Drake Boulevard, is a good place to start. There's parking at the beginning of Bolinas Avenue between Sir Francis Drake and Broadway. A block east on Broadway you'll see the Fairfax Theater, where the annual Thanksgiving Day mountain bike ride starts. Some of the cyclists who created the modern-day mountain bike live within riding distance of Fairfax.

Bolinas Avenue becomes Fairfax Bolinas Road when crossing San Anselmo Creek. Houses perched on poles cling to a canyon covered with toyon, bay laurel, poison oak, redwoods, and oaks. Near the summit you'll pass the Meadow Club Golf Course. The Marin water district maintains the gate on the road next to the golf course. They close the road on days when fire danger is high. Call (415) 924-4600 to check on the road's status.

Look for Alpine Lake far below from the first of two ridgetops. Pine Mountain Fire Truck Road on the right is one of the routes used for the Thanksgiving Day tour. As you look at the forested hillsides, note that this is all Marin County watershed. After an invigorating descent on the two-lane road, you'll wind through the redwoods to Alpine Lake dam, built in 1919.

The road climbs steadily through redwoods and

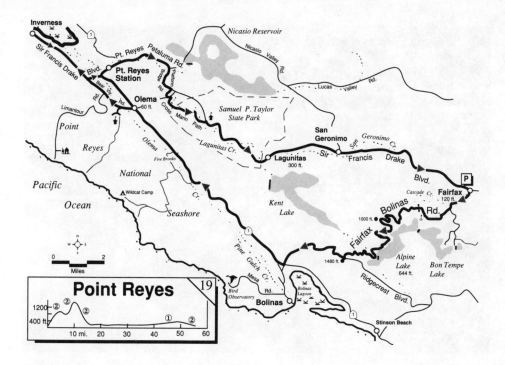

37.9 **Right** on Platform Bridge Road at stop sign.

40.2 **Right** at bike route sign just before Sir Francis Drake Boulevard stop sign and cross bridge over Lagunitas Creek.

40.3 **Left** onto Cross Marin recreation path. 42.5 Taylorville paper mill site.

43.5 **Left** over bridge to leave Samuel P. Taylor State Park at main entrance.

43.7 **Right** on Sir Francis Drake Boulevard at stop sign.

54.0 Fairfax. End ride.

Douglas fir from the dam to Bolinas Ridge. Turn right at the summit. Bolinas Ridge Trail on your right is described in another ride. Begin the descent to Highway 1. Poorly banked, bumpy corners will test your riding skills.

Highway 1 runs down the middle of San Andreas Valley, rolling over short hills, through groves of eucalyptus and green pastures. If it hasn't been stolen, you might see the Dogtown sign (population 30), bolted to a eucalyptus tree.

The town of Olema is a convenient place to stop for a snack. You're only a mile away from the Point Reyes National Seashore headquarters. The headquarters has a spacious interpretive center, restrooms, and water fountains.

The park was established in 1962, when about 64,000 acres was purchased; ranchers still lease Point Reyes land for cattle grazing. Point Reyes used to be part of Southern California, until it broke away and drifted slowly north over the past 100 million years or so. As Point Reyes continues its slow drift on the continental plate, it will reach Oregon in 50 million years, give or take 5 million years.

Fairfax Bolinas Road winds around Alpine Lake.

Exit park headquarters and head north to Inverness. On the way back, you'll visit Point Reyes Station before picking up Point Reyes–Petaluma Road about a half-mile outside town. Platform Bridge Road follows Lagunitas Creek to Sir Francis Drake Boulevard. Cross an old bridge over the creek before the stop sign, and immediately turn left onto the Cross Marin recreation path, which leads into Samuel P. Taylor State Park. The path was a right-of-way for the North Pacific Coast Railroad. You'll see a historical marker that records the site of the first paper mill west of the Mississippi. The mill was built by Samuel Taylor in 1856. Taylorville, a company town and health resort, sprang up along the banks of Lagunitas Creek.

Leave the park through the main entrance, and cross a bridge over the creek. You're back on Sir Francis Drake Boulevard, which passes through the villages of Lagunitas, Forest Knolls, and San Geronimo on the return to Fairfax. In 1992, a landslide at the summit of White's Hill temporarily blocked the road.

20 Tiburon and Golden Gate

Distance: 31 miles
Terrain: A few moderate hills
Traffic: Light to heavy

Biking around San Francisco Bay can be combined with a ferry trip to create a variety of different rides. This tour starts in San Francisco at the Golden Gate Bridge and goes to the village of Tiburon, where you can take the ferry back, visit Angel Island, or ride around Tiburon Peninsula.

Begin riding from a parking lot next to Battery Boutelle. The concrete fortress was built in 1901 and decommissioned at the end of World War II. None of the guns overlooking the Golden Gate ever fired at an enemy.

Crossing the Golden Gate Bridge is comparable to enjoying a fine meal at an exclusive restaurant. The views are "delicious" and they change with the weather, as do riding conditions. It can be windy, foggy, cloudy, clear, hot, cold, and any combination thereof.

People from throughout the Bay Area celebrated the bridge's fiftieth birthday on May 25, 1987, with extravagant fireworks and installation of permanent lighting for the span's twin towers. More than 50,000 people (the heaviest load supported by the bridge) jammed onto the 8,940-foot span, which remained closed to traffic for six hours. It took six years to build the bridge, and it cost $35 million and claimed the lives of 11 workers. It was the longest suspension bridge in the world at the time.

For your safety, obey these rules when crossing the bridge: You must ride on the west sidewalk on weekends and holidays, the east side on weekdays. Keep your speed down to 15 mph or less. Ride carefully, as it can be wet, cold, and windy at any time of year. Iron gratings on the sidewalk are slippery when wet. Use extreme caution when riding around the towers.

Follow signs from the parking lot to a path under

Mileage Log

0.0 Start mileage at coastal defense Battery Boutelle, on Merchant Road off Lincoln Boulevard and Highway 101.

0.1 Left and then immediate right into tunnel under Highway 101 and Golden Gate Bridge toll plaza. Ride through tunnel and turn left onto sidewalk immediately after exiting. 0.3 Ride over bridge on the east sidewalk weekdays, on the west sidewalk weekends. Take path under bridge to reach west side. 2.0 Bridge ends. If on the east sidewalk, ride into Vista Point parking lot, dismount and walk bike under Golden Gate Bridge on stairway and path. When you reach west side walk bike back up stairs and ride downhill on paved road under the bridge. If you started on west side, take first left through a gate, mile 1.7, and ride down Conzelman Road under bridge.

2.8 Right at stop sign. Ride through Fort Baker on Murray Circle.

3.0 Right on East Road.

3.8 Right merging onto Alexander Drive.

3.9 Right at junction onto Bridgeway with double-yellow street reflectors. 4.5 Downtown Sausalito. 5.8 Bay Model museum and display on right.

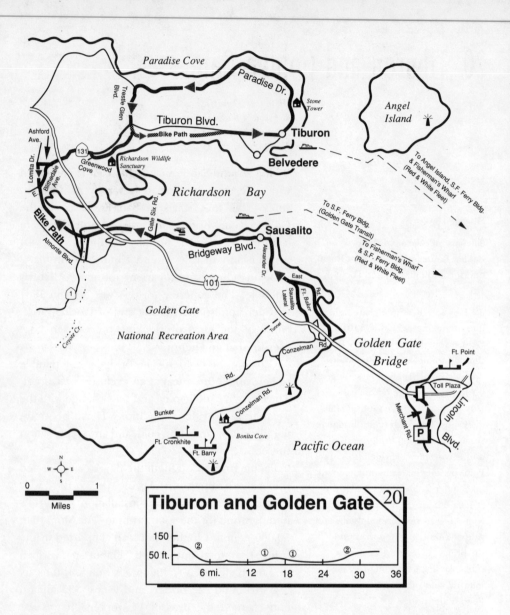

Paradise Cove

Paradise Dr.

Trestle Glen Blvd.

Tiburon Blvd.

Bike Path

Tiburon

Stone Tower

Angel Island

Ashford Ave.

131

Lomita Dr.

Blithedale Ave.

Greenwood Cove

Richardson Wildlife Sanctuary

Belvedere

Bike Path

Almonte Blvd.

Gate Six Rd.

Richardson Bay

To Angel Island, S.F. Ferry Bldg. & Fisherman's Wharf (Red & White Fleet)

To S.F. Ferry Bldg. (Golden Gate Transit)

To Fisherman's Wharf & S.F. Ferry Bldg. (Red & White Fleet)

Sausalito

Bridgeway Blvd.

Alexander Dr.

East

Ft. Baker Rd.

Sausalito Lateral

101

1

Coyote Cr.

Golden Gate

National Recreation Area

Tunnel

Conzelman Rd.

Golden Gate Bridge

Ft. Point

Toll Plaza

Merchant Rd.

Lincoln Blvd.

P

Rd.

Conzelman Rd.

Bunker

Ft. Cronkhite

Ft. Barry

Bonita Cove

Pacific Ocean

N W E S

0   1
Miles

Tiburon and Golden Gate 20

150
50 ft.

②   ①   ①   ②

6 mi.   12   18   24   30   36

6.8 Right onto bike path at freeway entrance and Gate Six Road. 7.6 Ride under Highway 101 overpass on path. 7.8 Cross bridge going north. 9.1 Drinking fountain. 9.2 Path ends. Begin East Blithedale Avenue at traffic light. 9.8 Highway 101 overpass. Blithedale becomes Tiburon Boulevard.

the bridge. It's an uphill ride the first half of the 1.7-mile span. On the northwest side, leave the bridge at a gate on your left, and go down the steep, paved Conzelman Road under the bridge (you can cut short the crossing by taking the first gate). On the northeast (bay side), enter the Vista Point parking lot, walk your bike down wooden stairs to a sidewalk under the bridge, and ride from a parking lot down to the road under the bridge. You'll pass Fort Baker, with its army houses lining a

10.6 Right on Greenwood Cove at traffic light, then take first left. Name changes to Greenwood Beach. 11.0 Richardson Bay Audubon Society Center and Sanctuary.

11.5 Right on path at end of Greenwood Beach. 11.6 Portable toilets. 11.9 Drinking fountain. 13.7 Path ends. Entering Tiburon on Main Street. 13.8 Downtown Tiburon. 14.0 Ferry dock for San Francisco and Angel Island. Golden Gate Transit (415) 453-2100 or Red & White Fleet (415) 546-2815. 14.4 Lyford stone tower. 17.3 Paradise Beach Park. Bicycles pay $1 to enter. Portable toilet, drinking fountains.

19.3 Left on Trestle Glen Boulevard. 19.9 Cross Tiburon Boulevard at traffic light and pick up path.

20.0 Left onto Greenwood Beach. Retrace route.

20.9 Left on Tiburon Boulevard at Greenwood Cove stoplight. 21.8 Highway 101 overpass.

22.2 Right on Ashford Street.

22.4 Left on Lomita Drive at stop sign. 22.6 Cross Blithedale at stoplight and pick up path on right. 24.2 Ride under Highway 101. 24.9 Sausalito Cyclery. Open seven days a week.

25.0 Left on Bridgeway at traffic light for Gate Six Road. 27.0 Downtown Sausalito. 27.9 Fort Baker exit on right if you choose to return this route. Or go straight as follows:

28.7 Left on recreation path. 29.0 View Point parking area. 29.1 Enter Golden Gate Bridge sidewalk. See Mile 0.3 for which side to ride on. 30.8 End bridge.

circular road. The Flying Wheels bicycle race was held here for many years.

There's a short, steep hill entering Sausalito. The town has two complexions depending on the time of week—quiet urban village on weekdays and crowded tourist haven on weekends.

The town's history dates back to 1838, when Captain William Richardson purchased a 19,000-acre Mexican land grant called Saucelito and built an adobe house at what is now Pine and Bonita streets. By the turn of the century the town had a ferry and a rail terminal.

In World War II, Sausalito was transformed from a colorful resort into a bustling shipyard. More than 30,000 shipbuilders worked around the clock at Marinship until it shut down in late 1945. They built 93 freighters and tankers. Local citizens want to build a Marinship museum next to the Army Corps of Engineers Bay Model on Bridgeway.

The Bay Model covers a two-acre warehouse and replicates San Francisco Bay. The U.S. Army Corps of Engineers built the hydraulic lab to study the bay. It's open from 9:00 A.M. to 4:00 P.M.. Tuesday through Saturday.

From Sausalito you can take a ferry to Fisherman's Wharf in San Francisco for less than $5, then cycle to your starting point (see San Francisco ride).

Leave Sausalito and take a path next to Bridgeway until Bridgeway merges with Highway 101. Wide, paved paths take you most of the way to the town of Tiburon. The path continues under massive columns supporting the Highway 101 overpass and follows the old right-of-way for the North Western Pacific Railroad through the wetlands. Houseboats next to the path are domesticated and have concrete foundations.

Tiburon was a busy rail terminal from 1884 until 1929. Peter Donahue, owner of the San Francisco and North Pacific Coast Railroad, and his son, James, extended the narrow-gauge line through Marin, Sonoma, and Napa counties.

You're about 14 miles from the Golden Gate. You can take the ferry to Angel Island (with a

Lyford stone tower near Tiburon was built for Dr. Benjamin Lyford.

30.9 Take tunnel under toll booths.

31.0 Right on Merchant Road at stop sign.

31.1 End ride.

paved path circling the island) or San Francisco, or continue on Paradise Drive.

Paradise Drive rolls gently around the peninsula. You won't miss the Lyford stone tower on Paradise Drive. It was built in 1889 by the San Francisco architect Gustav Behrnd for Dr. Benjamin F. Lyford, an embalming surgeon during the Civil War. Lyford moved West to regain his health at Tiburon, having made his fortune by being the first person to use makeup on corpses.

Lyford lived in a Victorian house on Greenwood Beach Road, conspicuous by its bright yellow exterior. It's now part of the Richardson Bay Wildlife Sanctuary and open to the public.

On the eastern shore of the peninsula, Paradise Beach County Park provides a good rest stop, with a view of San Pablo Strait. There's a restroom, picnic tables, a pier, and barbecue pits. All visitors must pay an entry fee.

Complete the peninsula loop by turning left on Trestle Glen Road and descending to Tiburon Boulevard. Retrace your route to complete the ride.

Road Rides

21 Calaveras Road

Distance: 37 miles
Terrain: One long moderate hill
Traffic: Light to moderate

Mileage Log

0.0 Start mileage at roadside picnic area at northeast corner of Highway 84 and Mission Boulevard. Ride east on Niles Canyon Road (Highway 84). 1.1 Railroad bridge over highway and Alameda Creek. 2.4 Narrow bridge. 3.0 Train tunnel. 3.4 Narrow bridge. Train tunnel on right.

5.9 Exit right into town of Sunol. Grocery store, post office, and gas station. 6.2 Ride through downtown Sunol.

6.3 Left at stop sign to return to Highway 84.

6.4 Right at stop sign. 7.2 Ride under Interstate 680. Calaveras Road begins. 7.4 Cork oak trees on right. 11.1 Alameda Creek. Begin climb. 14.0 False summit and meadow. 20.9 Summit. Begin steep descent.

21.2 Right on Calaveras Road at stop sign. 22.1 Ed Levin County Park. Drinking fountains and restrooms.

23.6 Right on Evans Road at bottom of hill. Name changes to North Park Victoria Boulevard at 24.9 miles.

26.4 Left on Scott Creek Road at stop sign. Ride under Interstate 680 at 26.5 miles.

27.0 Right on Warm Springs Boulevard at traffic light.

This ride has everything from computer factories to cork oak trees. The high point of the ride, literally and figuratively, comes on Calaveras Road, where you'll have views of the Bay Area's largest reservoir. The route also passes the former manufacturing plant for Apple Computers on Warm Springs Road.

Calaveras Road begins near Sunol and wends its way up to the ridge separating Santa Clara Valley from Sunol Valley. The road cuts through the San Francisco Water Department Hetch Hetchy watershed. Traffic is always light, and on Sunday mornings you may encounter only one or two cars.

Start riding from Vallejo Mill Park at the entrance to Niles Canyon in Fremont. The waterwheel-powered Vallejo Mill, imported from France, was located here. Don Jose de Jesus Vallejo operated the mill from 1853 until 1884. The roadside park has picnic tables and a commemorative plaque.

Niles Canyon Road follows Alameda Creek on a gentle uphill grade to Sunol. The railroad tracks on the north side of the canyon belonged to the now-defunct Southern Pacific, while the ones on the south side belong to the Union Pacific. The transcontinental railroad was built through the canyon in 1862, and the road was completed seven years later. Most of the day the two-lane road has moderate traffic, but it's heavy during commute hours.

If you want to ride through Sunol, exit right before the train subway. There's a food store if you're hungry. Continue through town and take a left at the stop sign to return to Highway 84.

The Hetch Hetchy pipeline passes a short distance south of Sunol. Look for a monument to the

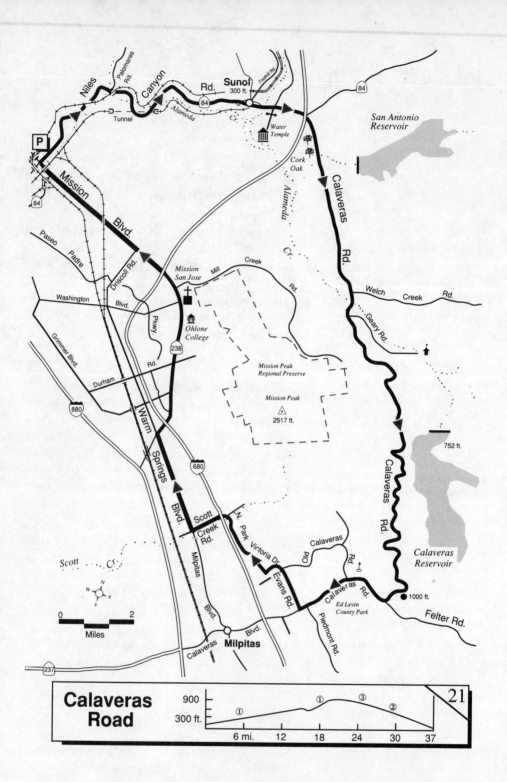

Niles

Palomares Rd.

Canyon Rd.

Sunol
300 ft.

Foothill Rd.

84

84

Tunnel

Alameda

Cr.

Water Temple

San Antonio Reservoir

P

Cork Oak

84

Mission Blvd.

Alameda Cr.

Calaveras Rd.

Paseo Padre

Driscoll Rd.

Mission San Jose

Mill Creek Rd.

Welch Creek Rd.

Washington Blvd.

Blvd.

Pkwy.

Ohlone College

Geary Rd.

Grimmer Blvd.

238

Rd.

Mission Peak Regional Preserve

Durham

Mission Peak
△ 2517 ft.

752 ft.

880

Warm Springs Blvd.

680

Scott Creek Rd.

N. Park Victoria Dr.

Calaveras Rd.

Calaveras Reservoir

Milpitas Blvd.

Evans Rd.

Pl O

Calaveras Rd.

1000 ft.

Scott Cr.

W
N
E
S

Calaveras Rd.

Ed Levin County Park

Felter Rd.

0   2
Miles

Piedmont Rd.

Calaveras Blvd.

Milpitas

237

Calaveras Road

900
300 ft.

① ③ ② ①

6 mi.   12   18   24   30   37

21

29.0 Right on Mission Boulevard at traffic light. Interstate 680 at 29.6 miles. 30.0 Mission Peak Regional Preserve entrance on right. 32.3 Mission San Jose de Guadalupe and Ohlone College on right. Food stores, gas stations, and restaurants nearby.

36.5 Right on Highway 84 at traffic light.

36.6 **Left** at roadside parking area. End of ride.

aqueduct on your right in an onion field as you pass the junction of Highway 84 and Pleasanton-Sunol Road. The water temple's impressive Roman columns replicate another temple north of Woodside on Cañada Road.

Calaveras Road begins at the stop sign just past Interstate 680. Don't miss the cork oak trees on the right next to the road. Cross Alameda Creek, and the climb begins. The road has infrequent washouts after heavy rains.

Calaveras Reservoir dominates the scene as you near the ridgetop. Spring Valley Water Works built the dam in 1925. The water company was purchased by the San Francisco Water Department shortly after the dam's completion. A pipeline under the Bay, connecting the Alameda Creek reservoir system with San Francisco, dates back to 1888.

The character of the ride changes from country-side to urban hussle and bustle in Milpitas and north to Fremont. However, Evans Road and North Park Victoria Drive avoid most of the traffic.

On Mission Boulevard you'll see Mission San Jose de Guadalupe. When the Spaniards settled the region, they built a series of missions from San Diego to San Francisco. The one-story building on Mission is made from dried mud, or adobe; the church is made from stone. The mission museum is open daily 10:00 A.M. to 4:00 P.M. The mission was founded in 1797 by Francisco de Lausen. Kit Carson, the famed explorer, is known to have visited the mission, along with another icon of the Old West, the fur trapper Jedediah Smith, in 1827.

22 Clayton

Distance: 53 miles
Terrain: Moderately hilly
Traffic: Light to heavy

This ride circles the volcano-shaped Mt. Diablo, giving you a view of the familiar and not so familiar. Especially stunning are the steep, rocky slopes of the eastern face. There's also a memorable climb on the secluded Morgan Territory Road.

Start at the base of Mt. Diablo in the town of Danville, off Interstate 680. Danville was a farm community until the 1950s, when improved water service brought rapid growth. The town was named for the first settlers to the area in 1852, brothers Daniel and Andrew Inman. Some of the town's history is preserved at the Southern Pacific train depot on Railroad Avenue next to where the ride begins. The weathered wooden building stands as a reminder of the simpler days of the iron horse.

Ride northwest on Hartz Avenue from the California Pedaler bike shop. The road to Walnut Creek has a wide shoulder and bike lanes, with moderate to light traffic. Danville Road follows a former stagecoach route between Martinez and San Jose, passing century-old ranches and acres of walnut orchards. The scenery is best in the late winter, when yellow mustard carpets the orchards. Oddly enough, wheat was grown here in the late 1880s, to be replaced by vineyards and fruit orchards.

The mood and scenery changes in Walnut Creek, where traffic is heavy most weekdays and even on weekends. The modern city's glass and steel buildings dwarf the older brick structures you'll see on Main Street.

In contrast to the busy streets of downtown Walnut Creek, Contra Costa Canal shines like a recreational gem. There's a paved path following the canal into woodsy neighborhoods. Watch out for pedestrians, roller skaters, skateboarders, and

Mileage Log

0.0 Start mileage at the intersection of Church Street and South Hartz Avenue, next to California Pedaler bike shop, 295 South Hartz Avenue. Phone (510) 820-0345. Ride north on South Hartz Avenue, which becomes North Hartz and then Danville Boulevard. 5.0 Walnut Creek city limits sign. 5.5 Interstate 680 overpass. 5.9 Main Street.

6.7 Right on Civic Drive at traffic light.

8.2 Right on Contra Costa Canal recreation trail. Watch for the yellow road sign that says Trail Crossing.

11.3 Left at junction over Contra Costa Canal bridge.

11.7 Right on Treat Boulevard.

13.5 Right on Clayton Road at traffic light.

17.1 Right on Marsh Creek Road at traffic light.

18.1 Keep right on Marsh Creek Road at traffic light for second time. 19.6 Rodie's Store. Last chance for food or drink until Danville.

21.5 Right on Morgan Territory Road. In 4 miles road narrows. 30.7 Morgan Territory Regional Preserve parking area on left. Restrooms, hiking, off-road riding available. 31.0 Summit. Begin descent to Manning Road.

Road Rides

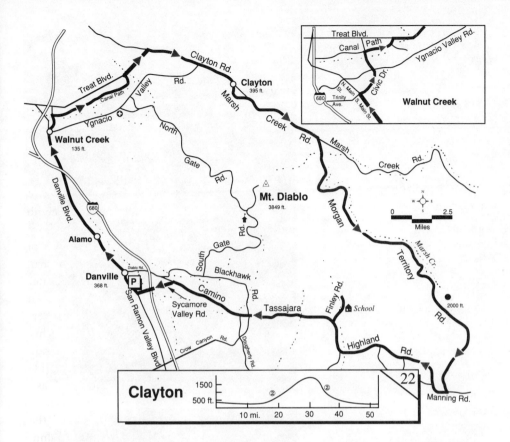

Clayton

22

36.1 Right on Manning Road at stop sign.

37.0 Right on Highland Road at stop sign.

41.7 Right on Camino Tassajara at stop sign.

43.0 Right on Finley Road. 43.6 Old Tassajara School. Return.

44.2 Right on Camino Tassajara at stop sign.

50.3 Left on Sycamore Valley Road at Camino Tassajara junction.

51.8 Right on San Ramon Valley Boulevard at stoplight, just after crossing Interstate 680 overpass. Becomes North Hartz Avenue.

52.5 End ride at Church Street.

other cyclists using the path, and use caution crossing busy streets. You'll leave the canal at Treat Boulevard and ride south on Clayton Road, a wide avenue lined with retail stores.

Though urban sprawl has slowed considerably in the Bay Area, a final bastion in what was once a rural setting has fallen. Clayton Road takes you to the town of Clayton. Joel Clayton, a San Francisco dairyman, founded the town. Coal and copper mines in the nearby hills gave residents a modest livelihood until the late 1800s, when vineyards and wineries sprang up. Town center has been preserved, but surrounded as it is by modern subdivisions, the town resembles a movie set, its wooden buildings so much simulacrum.

Outside Clayton, the rocky spire of Mt. Diablo's eastern face reveals itself. Legend has it that local resident Jeremiah Morgan "discovered" this rugged area in 1856 while hunting on Mt. Diablo.

Morgan Territory Road rises to 2,000 feet for a spectacular overlook of San Ramon Valley.

A historic one-room schoolhouse on Finley Road recalls simpler days.

Ranch land on Highland Road is giving way to development.

As he looked out over the hills he declared all the land in view to be his, about 10,000 acres' worth.

Turn right on Morgan Territory Road, where you'll enter a wide valley that soon narrows. The road snakes uphill, following Marsh Creek under a canopy of oaks. It's a steady climb up to 2,000 feet, with only a couple of short, steep pitches. At the summit you're rewarded with a spectacular view of ranch lands to the west and south. After a brisk descent to Manning Road, the ride is mostly flat to Danville. Don't miss Tassajara School on Finley Road. Rows of majestic walnut trees give welcome shade to the one-room school. The bell tower and turnstile were common features for schools built in 1888.

Return to Danville on Camino Tassajara Road, which passes "executive homes" in the Blackhawk development. Residents spare no expense at making themselves visibly comfortable. For example, one house is touted to have 13 color televisions, a baby grand piano, a swimming pool, and enough remote controls for stereos and VCRs to supply Malibu. The Blackhawk developer lives in a 30,000-square-foot residence with wall-to-wall sound that includes 105 stereo speakers.

23 East Bay Hills

Distance: 28 miles
Terrain: Hilly
Traffic: Light to moderate

Mileage Log

0.0 Start mileage at Inspiration Point in Tilden Regional Park at the summit of Wildcat Canyon Road. No services here. Turn left from parking lot and begin descent.

2.4 Right on Camino Pablo Road at traffic light. 4.5 Ride under Highway 24 overpass. Camino Pablo becomes Moraga Way. 4.6 Downtown Orinda on left at Brookwood Road.

9.2 Right on Canyon Road at traffic light.

11.0 Left at Pinehurst Road junction and stop sign, beginning climb. Right goes steeply uphill to Skyline Boulevard. 12.2 Alameda County line. 12.5 Summit. Begin 1.2-mile descent.

13.7 Right on Redwood Road at stop sign. Begin 4-mile climb.

16.1 Right on Skyline Boulevard at traffic light.

16.7 Keep right on Skyline Boulevard at junction with Joaquin Miller Road. 17.7 Summit.

19.4 Keep right at junction with Carlsbrook Drive. 19.8 Water fountain on right at parking lot for Skyline Gate staging area in Redwood Regional Park.

20.2 Shallow left at Pinehurst Road junction, staying on Skyline.

Despite a devastating fire here on October 20, 1991, a ride through the Oakland hills offers uncompromising views of San Francisco Bay, its bridges, and San Francisco. During the ups and downs in this hilly ride, you'll see everything from charred hillsides to lush redwood groves and elegant rural communities. The fire that ravaged the Oakland hills claimed 25 lives and destroyed almost 3,000 houses and apartments. This was the most costly urban fire in United States history. Damage estimates run as high as $1 billion. That fateful Saturday the weather followed the pattern firefighters fear most—low humidity, strong easterly winds, high temperatures, and parched ground.

It will be years, perhaps decades, before the scars disappear. Because the fire swept downhill toward densely populated Oakland and Berkeley, Skyline Boulevard and the nearby regional parks were spared. Most roads reopened shortly after the fire.

The aptly named Inspiration Point in Tilden Regional Park offers a convenient location to start the ride. Go left from the parking lot, and descend the two-lane Wildcat Canyon Road. Turn right at the bottom of the hill on Camino Pablo, and continue through Orinda to the town of Moraga. Traffic can be moderate to heavy, but the two-lane road has a wide shoulder and gentle climbs and descents. The reason Moraga Way has gentle climbs is because it was built as a railroad right-of-way in 1889. The California and Nevada line was derailed by financial troubles, however, and couldn't be extended to the town.

The town of Orinda, at the intersection of Camino Pablo and Highway 24, is served by BART. The intersection was formerly called The Crossroads because two of the region's oldest main

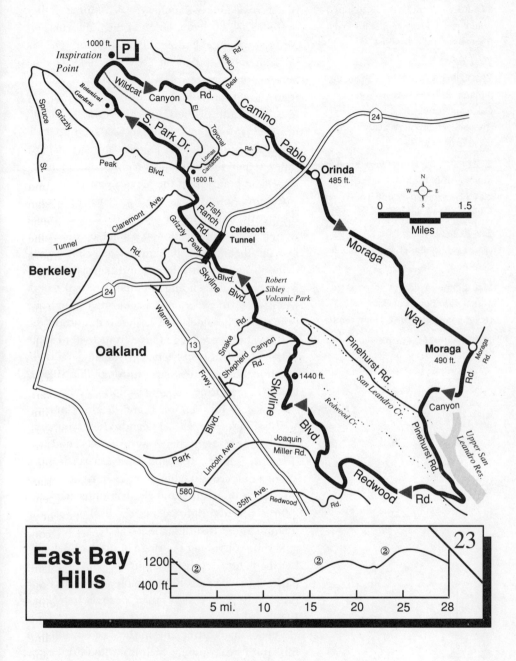

1000 ft.　P

Inspiration Point

Wildcat
Canyon　Rd.

Bear
Creek
Rd.

Camino
Pablo

24

Orinda
485 ft.

N
W · E
S

0 ——————— 1.5
Miles

*Botanical
Gardens*

Spruce

Grizzly

St.

Peak

S. Park Dr.

Blvd.

El Toyonal

Lomas
Cantadas

1600 ft.

Fish
Ranch
Rd.

Grizzly Peak

Claremont　Ave.

Tunnel

Rd.

Berkeley

24

Warren

Caldecott
Tunnel

Skyline

Blvd.

Blvd.

*Robert
Sibley
Volcanic Park*

Moraga

Way

Moraga
490 ft.

Moraga
Rd.

Oakland

13

Frwy.

Snake

Rd.

Shepherd Canyon

Rd.

Skyline

Blvd.

1440 ft.

Pinehurst Rd.

San Leandro Cr.

Redwood Cr.

Pinehurst Rd.

Canyon

Rd.

Upper San
Leandro Res.

Park

Blvd.

Lincoln Ave.

Joaquin
Miller Rd.

580

35th Ave.

Redwood

Rd.

Redwood

Rd.

East Bay
Hills

1200

400 ft.

②

②

②

5 mi.　10　15　20　25　28

23

20.8 Keep right at Snake Road junction. Begin 1.3-mile climb. 21.7 Water fountain on right at Robert Sibley park entrance.

21.8 Right on Grizzly Peak Road. 22.1 Summit. Road levels. Cross over Caldecott Tunnel. 22.4 View of Bay Area on left; 23.5 view. 24.0 Begin 0.2-mile descent.

24.2 Straight on Grizzly Peak Road at four-way stop. Begin 1.4-mile climb. 25.4 Steam train park on right. Water fountain at entrance.

25.6 Right on South Park Road, crossing train tunnel. Begin 1.5-mile descent.

27.1 Right on Wildcat Canyon Road at stop sign. Botanical Gardens straight ahead. Begin 1.2-mile climb.

28.3 End of ride at Inspiration Point.

roads crossed here. Ranchers settled Moraga Valley in the 1870s. The completion of the California and Nevada rail line between Berkeley and Orinda brought more settlers in 1890. In 1903, Orinda became even less isolated from Oakland when a road tunnel was completed through the East Bay hills, just south of the Caldecott Tunnel. The old tunnel was closed in 1937 when Caldecott opened.

Moraga was named for Joaquin Moraga, an early valley settler in 1835 who received one of many large land grants from the Mexican government.

Continue on Moraga Way, and turn right onto the lightly traveled Canyon Road. The shopping center at the intersection was built by developer Donald Rheem in 1950. Canyon Road climbs gradually through open hillsides and a grove of eucalyptus before descending to Pinehurst Road, where you're likely to experience a cool ride through the redwoods. The oldest and largest redwoods in the East Bay hills were logged here from 1840 to 1860. (The ride can be shortened by turning right on Pinehurst Road, which passes through the "village" of Canyon, a former logging camp.)

Turn left on Pinehurst and begin climbing. You'll soon see Upper San Leandro Reservoir, built in 1926. Turn right at Redwood Road. Food and drink are sold at Redwood Lodge, a rustic store about a mile from the junction. Turn right, staying on Skyline Boulevard, and climb another half-mile before bearing right again on Skyline, at the Joaquin Miller Road junction.

Skyline rolls along the ridge of the East Bay hills between housing developments and regional parks. After passing Robert Sibley Volcanic Park, don't miss a key right turn onto Grizzly Peak Boulevard.

One of many attractions in the East Bay hills is a miniature steam train, which is located just before South Park Drive. Train rides can be taken from 11:00 A.M. to 6:00 P.M. on weekends year-around, 1:00 P.M. to 6:00 P.M. on weekdays during spring and summer school vacations. Phone (510) 548-6100.

Tilden Regional Park's miniature train attracts riders of all ages.

A quarter-mile past the train, turn right and begin a steep descent on South Park Drive. If you're taking this ride between November and March, the road is closed to all but bicycles. Turn right at Wildcat Canyon Road and ride back to Inspiration Point. In 1992 the East Bay Regional Park District started closing South Park Drive to cars during the winter to keep newts from being squished. Many slow-moving brownish red salamanders cross the road to reach their mating grounds.

Near the end of the ride you'll pass the Botanical Gardens. The park replicates California's diverse vegetation and contains almost every plant native to the state. Hours are 10:00 A.M. to 5:00 P.M.

One way to celebrate the finish is to have a picnic at Inspiration Point. Walk or ride north on Nimitz Way, where you can watch the sun set behind the Golden Gate Bridge from the peaceful vantage point of a former Nike missile bunker.

24 East Bay Reservoirs

Distance: 23 miles
Terrain: Moderately hilly
Traffic: Light

Mileage Log

0.0 Start mileage at Highway 24 overpass. If driving, park in Orinda, or take BART to Orinda. Ride northwest on Camino Pablo.

2.1 Right on Bear Creek Road at traffic light. Two climbs to Briones Regional Park. 6.5 Briones Regional Park entrance on right. Two climbs to Alhambra Valley Road.

10.7 Left on Alhambra Valley Road at stop sign.

13.4 Left on Castro Ranch Road.

15.7 Left on San Pablo Dam Road at traffic light. 21.1 Bear Creek Road junction.

23.2 Ride under Highway 24. Ride ends.

If you've ridden on the crowded streets of Berkeley or Oakland, the wide-open spaces of the East Bay watershed bring welcome relief. The original Rancho El Sobrante land grant has turned into a veritable "Rancho La Bicicleta." Hundreds of riders tour the open spaces on fair-weather weekends.

The watershed's lands were purchased from Mexico in 1841 by Victor and Juan Castro. (*Sobrante* is Spanish for "vacant" or "remaining.") Squatters quickly moved onto the Castro property, and before long the land was parceled out. In 1868, a son of one of the Castros built a ranch at the intersection of Castro Ranch Road and San Pablo Dam Road.

Start the ride in downtown Orinda, loop around Briones and San Pablo dams, and return to town. As you ride under the busy Highway 24 overpass, imagine what life was like here in 1941, when this intersection had the distinction of acquiring the first traffic light in the area. San Pablo Dam Road wasn't paved until 1919. In 1952 it was widened and straightened to its present alignment. The only evidence of a building boom in the valley comes on Castro Ranch Road, where subdivisions have been built near the top of the short climb. In contrast, the ranches and hay fields in Alhambra Valley still see little traffic.

A challenging climb greets you on Bear Creek Road. It can be unpleasantly hot on summer days, so plan your ride accordingly. Bear Creek Road rolls up and down on the way to Alhambra Valley Road, with two major but gradual climbs.

The watershed's dams were built during World War I. As early as the 1890s, local residents envisioned a dam on San Pablo Creek for irrigation. Construction began in 1916 and took three years using horse-drawn scrapers. San Pablo Dam was

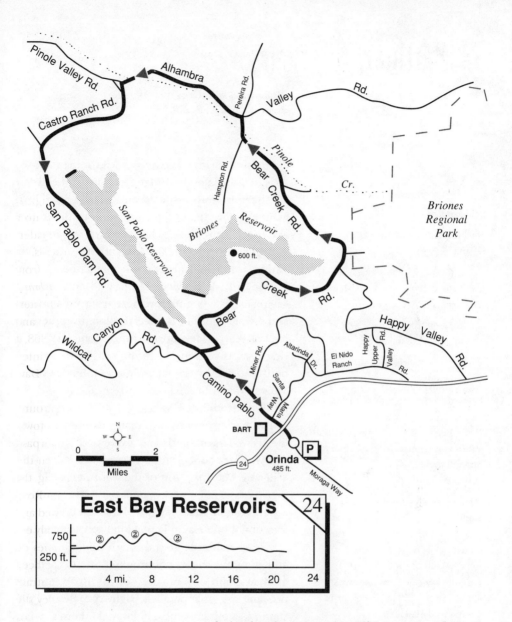

East Bay Reservoirs

drained and reinforced in 1979 at a cost of $15 million to meet state earthquake standards.

The reservoir contains water from the creek and the Sierra Nevada. After a disastrous drought in 1918, a pipeline was built from the Mokelumne River in the Sierra Nevada. The East Bay Municipal Utility District project was completed in 1929, just in time to avert another water shortage.

25 Martinez

Distance: 18 miles
Terrain: A few gentle hills
Traffic: Light

Mileage Log

0.0 Start mileage at John Muir House.

0.1 Right on Franklin Canyon Road. 3.0 Begin gradual climb. 3.7 McEwen Road at right.

4.5 Right on Cummings Skyway at stop sign. 6.0 Summit.

6.6 Right on Crockett Boulevard, beginning descent.

8.6 Right at stop sign on Pomona Street. Becomes Carquinez Scenic Drive. Begin 0.6 mile climb. 10.3 Bull Valley Staging Area for Carquinez Strait Shoreline.

11.4 Keep straight at three-way junction. Steep hill on right goes to Highway 4. 12.5 Gate. Road closed past this point. Rock crushing yard on left. 13.3 Gate. 14.2 Gate. 16.0 John Nejedly Staging Area. 16.4 Carquinez Scenic Drive becomes Talbart Street. Talbart Street turns left in residential area.

16.5 Right on Berrellessa Street at stop sign. One way. 17.3 Becomes Alhambra Valley Road.

18.3 Ride ends at John Muir House.

Carquinez Bridge, spanning Carquinez Strait, reflected the latest in bridge technology when built in 1927. Its impressive steel girders resemble a giant Erector set. On this ride you'll see the bridge and much more in the Martinez-Crockett area.

Begin the ride in Martinez at the John Muir House, a national historic site maintained by the National Park Service. Muir, who was one of California's first and foremost environmentalists and a co-founder of the Sierra Club, lived here in his last years. (He's buried in the cemetery you'll ride past as you enter Martinez.) The house was built in 1882 by his father-in-law, John Strentzel. Muir moved into the house in 1890 and lived there until his death in 1914.

The park grounds have many varieties of plant life, as well as orchards and a vineyard. Don't miss the Martinez adobe in the rear of the estate. Don Vincente Martinez, son of the *commandante* of the Presidio of San Francisco, built the house of adobe bricks around 1848. It's the oldest dwelling in the area and a fine example of adobe construction.

The 18-mile ride goes through Alhambra Valley and along the shores of Carquinez Strait. There's a gradual climb on Franklin Canyon Road, a quiet two-lane road that parallels Highway 4. Beyond the summit, after crossing Highway 4, there's a fast downhill on Crockett Boulevard.

The most enjoyable section of the ride comes on Carquinez Scenic Drive. The road was closed by landslides in the 1970s. However, it's open for bicycling and hiking. Short sections of road are unpaved. You'll have excellent views of the strait as well as the Southern Pacific rail line that hugs the shore.

Even though it's at the fringe of the sprawling East Bay, Martinez retains its small-town charm.

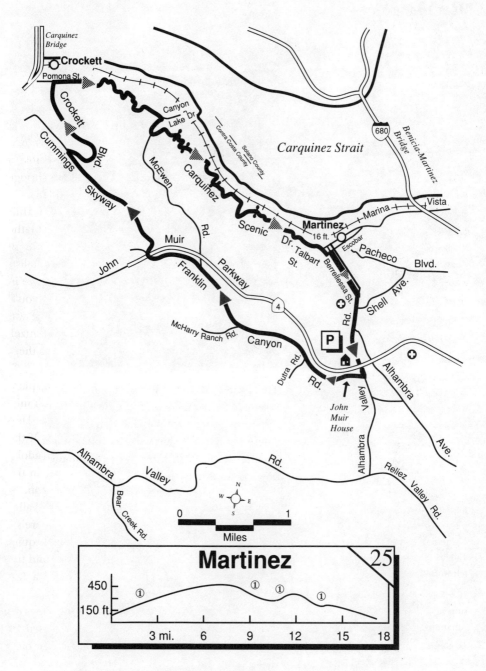

*Carquinez Bridge comes into view during
the descent on Crockett Boulevard.*

The town's narrow, hilly streets next to the bay
resemble San Francisco. At the turn of the century
the town was a commercial transportation hub.
There was a nearby ferry service and a stagecoach.
The well-known Alhambra Water Company started
bottling water here in 1903.

26 Mt. Diablo

Distance: 29 miles
Terrain: Hilly
Traffic: Light to moderate

Mileage Log

0.0 Start mileage in Danville on corner of Church Street and South Hartz Avenue next to California Pedaler bike shop at 295 South Hartz Avenue. Phone (510) 820-0345. Ride north on South Hartz Avenue, which becomes North Hartz Avenue.

0.2 Right on Diablo Road at traffic light. 0.5 Interstate 680 underpass.

0.8 Keep left on Diablo Road at Camino Tassajara junction.

1.3 Right at traffic light, continuing on Diablo Road.

1.9 Keep right on Diablo Road at Green Valley Road junction. Diablo Road changes name to Blackhawk Road.

3.4 Left on Mt. Diablo Scenic Boulevard. Look for green sign and two stone columns. Name changes to South Gate Road. 7.4 South Gate park entrance.

9.7 Right on Summit Road at ranger station. 14.3 Summit. Return same route.

28.6 End of ride.

Bicyclists have been riding up Mt. Diablo to its 3,489-foot summit ever since a toll road was built in 1879. Today, the ride is one of the most challenging and popular climbs in the Bay Area. Most times of the year tour groups make the trip up, and there's the occasional race. The satisfaction gained from conquering the mountain is reason enough to ride up it. But on a clear day the view from the summit brings its own reward. You can see the Farallon Islands, Mt. Shasta, the Sierra, and Monterey Bay.

The mountain began drawing vacationers in the late 1800s when the Mt. Diablo Summit Road Company built a 16-room hotel 3 miles from the summit. One of the builders, R. N. Burgess, was no stranger to mountain chalets. He had previously owned a hotel on 6,000-foot Mt. Washington in New Hampshire.

In 1891, the summit observation platform burned, the hotel suffering the same fate soon afterward. The toll road was closed and didn't reopen until 1915. In 1921 a parcel of land on Mt. Diablo was dedicated to become a state park, and over the years the park has been expanded to include more than 15,000 acres.

You'll start riding from downtown Danville and take the south summit road, one of two approach roads into the park. The roads join 4.6 miles from the summit at a ranger station.

After riding through several miles of urban setting, turn left at the south park entrance, identifiable by two small stone columns and an unobtrusive sign. The road hugs the side of the mountain, winding upward at a steady grade of about 6 percent. In the spring the pleasant aroma of buckbrush permeates the fresh, cool air. Park maps are available at the gate. Bicyclists enter for free.

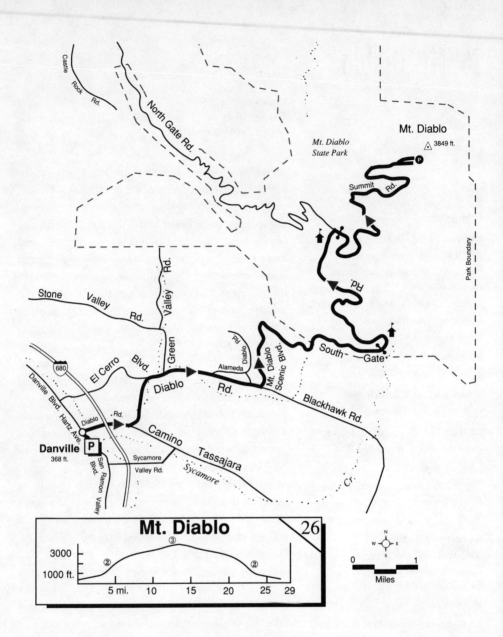

Castle Rock Rd.

North Gate Rd.

Mt. Diablo State Park

Mt. Diablo

△ 3849 ft.

P

Summit Rd.

Rd.

Park Boundary

Stone Valley Rd.

Green Valley Rd.

El Cerro Blvd.

680

Danville Blvd.

Hartz Ave.

Diablo Rd.

Diablo Rd.

Rd.

Alameda

Mt. Diablo Scenic Blvd.

South Gate

Diablo Rd.

Blackhawk Rd.

Camino Tassajara

Danville
368 ft.

P

San Ramon Valley Blvd.

Sycamore Valley Rd.

Sycamore

Cr.

Mt. Diablo

26

3000

1000 ft.

③

②

②

5 mi.   10   15   20   25   29

N
W   E
S

0   1

Miles

Notice the rock outcropping, called Fossil Ridge, near the south entrance ranger station. The sedimentary rock was pushed up with the rest of Mt. Diablo millions of years ago, exposing the fossilized remains of shellfish, mastadons, and saber-toothed tigers.

Turn right at the ranger station junction. The road steepens from here. You'll see Livermore Valley and Mt. Hamilton in the distance. Just before you reach the summit, there's a parking lot on the right where the road branches. Keep right on the narrow one-way road that steepens to a breathtaking 18 percent for the next 300 yards! Return the way you came, but take the other one-way road leaving the parking lot.

It gets hot on Mt. Diablo in the summer, so start your ride early. Water fountains are located at the south ranger station and the main park office at the junction. Many campsites along the road have restrooms. There's a drinking fountain and a restroom at the summit, but the food stand inside the stone building shut down long ago. For more information, write to Mt. Diablo State Park, P.O. Box 250, Diablo, CA 94528. Phone (510) 837-2525.

27 Sunol

Distance: 28 miles
Terrain: Several gradual hills
Traffic: Light to moderate

Mileage Log

0.0 Start mileage at Sunol General Store. Ride west on Highway 84 (Niles Canyon Road).

4.2 Right on Palomares Road immediately after railroad bridge. 7.5 Westover vineyard. 7.7 Chouinard Winery and Vineyard. 8.6 Summit.

13.7 Right on Palo Verde Road at stop sign.

14.1 Right on Dublin Canyon Road at stop sign. 19.2 Name changes to Foothill Road in Pleasanton.

24.0 Left on Castlewood Drive at stop sign if you return on Pleasanton Sunol Road. (Otherwise, continue on Foothill Road.) Right again onto Pleasanton Sunol Road after crossing bridge. Right on Niles Canyon Road, cross Arroyo de la Laguna, and then right again to return to Sunol.

27.5 End ride in Sunol.

I call this East Bay tour the "Ride of Three Canyons"—Niles, Stonybrook, and Dublin. You'll make a loop through scenic countryside past famous rail lines, two little-known wineries, and the western edge of Amador Valley.

Start the tour in Sunol, a rural community near Niles Canyon Road (Highway 84) and Interstate 680. The one-street town takes life with an easygoing sense of humor. At one time their honorary mayor was Bosco, a 70-pound Labrador retriever who, from time to time, wandered off and was not seen for weeks.

Sunol may make light of its mayor, but it takes its trains seriously. It's home to the Niles Canyon Scenic Railroad, a collection of steam locomotives owned by the Pacific Locomotive Association. The association has rebuilt more than 2 miles of abandoned Southern Pacific track on the north side of Niles Canyon, where the transcontinental railroad track was laid. They plan to extend the track 9 miles, from Vallejo Mills Park in Fremont to a point outside Pleasanton. Rides are open to the public the first and third Sunday every month. For more information, write to Pacific Locomotive Association, P.O. Box 2247, Fremont, CA 94536, or phone (510) 862-9063.

Ride west down Niles Canyon Road a couple of miles and turn right on Palomares Road, just after the train bridge. Traffic is moderate in Niles Canyon on weekends, heavy on weekdays during commute hours. Palomares Road has little traffic in secluded Stonybrook Canyon. Sycamore, madrone, dense growths of poison oak, and buckeye line the road.

Several miles up the road, you'll pass Westover Vineyard and Chouinard Winery and vineyard,

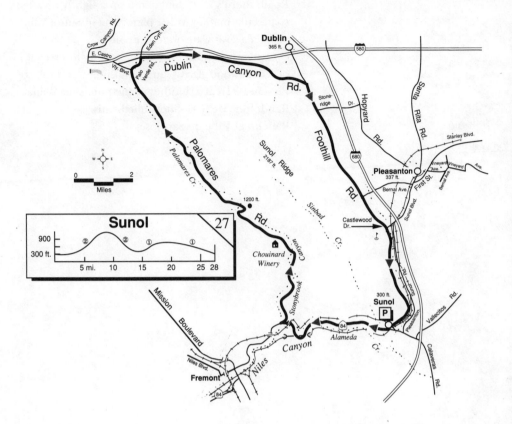

owned by the Chouinard family. They offer wine tastings on weekends. Some wine is made from the on-site vineyard, which was planted in 1979. For more information, call (510) 582-9900.

Climb for several miles, and then start a brisk descent into a valley with horse ranches, white picket fences, and cherry orchards. Leave Palomares Road and enter Dublin Canyon on Dublin Canyon Road, which parallels Interstate 580. There's a 2-mile climb followed by a 2-mile descent into Pleasanton.

The ride complexion changes from rural canyons to housing developments and modern office buildings in Amador Valley. Dublin Canyon Road becomes Foothill Road in Pleasanton.

You have two options for riding to Sunol; take Foothill or Pleasanton Sunol Road next to Arroyo de la Laguna. If you return to Sunol on Foothill

Road, there's a gradual climb on a lightly traveled road, culminating with a panorama of Sunol Valley and Calaveras Canyon to the south.

Castlewood Country Club, at the intersection of Castlewood Drive and Foothill, was built by Phoebe A. Hearst, mother of the publisher William Randolph Hearst. She called this lavish resort Rancho el Valle de San Jose.

28 Atherton and Menlo Park

Distance: 13 miles
Terrain: A few easy hills
Traffic: Moderate to light

Mileage Log

0.0 Start mileage at corner of Mielke Drive and Alma Street. Parking available at Burgess Park. Ride northeast on Mielke to Laurel Street.

0.1 Left on Laurel Street at stop sign.

0.2 Left on Ravenswood Avenue at traffic light. Becomes Menlo Avenue.

0.8 Left on University Drive at stop sign.

1.1 Right on Middle Avenue at stop sign.

1.8 Right on Olive Street at stop sign.

1.9 Left again on Oakdell Drive in short distance.

2.5 Left on Santa Cruz Avenue at stop sign.

2.7 Left at traffic light, staying on Santa Cruz Avenue.

3.0 Right on Sand Hill Road at traffic light. Begin 1.1-mile climb. 3.8 Stanford Linear Accelerator entrance. 4.7 Interstate 280 overpass. 4.9 Begin 0.5-mile climb.

6.0 Right on Whiskey Hill Road.

7.3 Right on Woodside Road, Highway 84, at stop sign.

8.5 Right on Northgate Drive immediately after flashing sign Signal Ahead.

8.9 Left on Stockbridge Avenue.

9.8 Right on Euclid Avenue.

In the late 1800s, the towns of Atherton and Menlo Park became popular summer retreats for San Francisco's wealthy. Southern Pacific Railroad owners Leland Stanford, Collis Huntington, Charles Crocker, and Mark Hopkins built magnificent estates here. They were joined by mining tycoon Jim Flood, William Ralston, and spice baron August Schilling.

Today Atherton's quiet, tree-lined streets retain their historic and rural character. Financiers, businessmen, entertainers, and sports legends live here in relative seclusion.

Start the ride at Menlo Park City Hall, next to Burgess Park. Ride northeast on Mielke, and turn left on Laurel Street. The ride takes you through downtown Menlo Park, past the swank Drager's grocery store, where you might see some luminaries shopping if you stop for a cup of cappuccino at the upstairs café.

Sand Hill Road takes you from an urban to a rural setting. The four-lane divided road turns to two lanes with wide shoulders past Interstate 280. On the way, you'll ride by the entrance to the Stanford Linear Accelerator, where scientists conduct research on subatomic particles. Electrons are accelerated to nearly the speed of light down a long chamber into a storage ring at the end, where controlled collisions between electrons and positrons create even smaller particles.

Sand Hill Road is one of the oldest logging roads in the area, dating back to the days of the Spanish settlers in the early 1800s. Later it became a stage route. Although the Spanish used mostly clay for building material, they needed wood for roofing and framework. True to its name, the road is built on loose sandstone. As late as the 1930s, before the

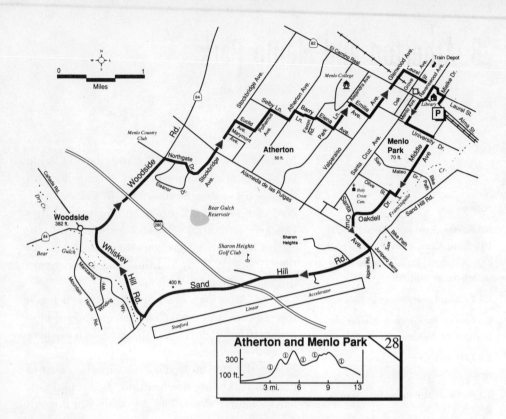

Atherton and Menlo Park 28

10.0 Left on Polhemus Avenue at T intersection.

10.4 Right on Selby Lane at stop sign.

10.7 Left on Atherton Avenue at stop sign.

10.8 Right on Barry Lane.

11.0 Left on Faxon Road at stop sign.

11.1 Right on Elena Avenue at stop sign.

11.3 Left on Park Lane at stop sign.

11.7 Right on Emilie Avenue at stop sign.

12.0 Left on Valparaiso Avenue at stop sign.

12.6 Right on Laurel Street at stop sign.

13.2 Right on Mielke Drive. End ride.

road was paved, cars became stuck in the sand. A scene from the movie *Harold and Maude* was filmed at the top of the hill to the right.

Jasper Ridge Biological Preserve occupies wooded land to the southwest and is visible from the top of Sand Hill Road. Every Northern California plant habitat can be found on the 1,200-acre Stanford University nature preserve. The habitat was established in the 1960s, and its recreation facilities were closed to the public in the 1970s.

Turn right on Whiskey Hill Road and climb a short hill. At the stop sign on Woodside Road, turn right and begin the descent to Northgate Drive. Turn right and climb some more on quiet, residential streets. Follow the map carefully in Atherton. Many of the road signs consist of short white posts.

29 Hillsborough

Distance: 13 miles
Terrain: One long hill
Traffic: Light

Mileage Log

0.0 Start mileage at the intersection of East Fifth Avenue and South B Street in downtown San Mateo. Talbot's Bike Shop is located on the corner. Ride west on East Fifth Avenue 0.1 Japanese garden and tennis courts on left at Laurel Avenue. Follow path through park to see garden behind high wooden fence.

0.4 Right on Dartmouth Road at stop sign. Note giant bay tree.

0.5 Dartmouth jogs left. Cross West Third Avenue at stop light. Location of the Portola expedition along San Mateo Creek. Turn around.

0.7 Right on West Third Avenue at traffic light.

0.8 Right on Eaton Road.

0.9 Left on Crystal Springs Road at stop sign.

1.6 Left at stop sign, staying on Crystal Springs Road.

3.3 Right, staying on Crystal Springs Road at Polhemus Road junction.

4.2 Right on Skyline Boulevard at stop sign.

5.4 Right on Hayne Road at stop sign. 5.6 Go straight at stop sign.

5.7 Left on Darrell Road, around circle.

5.9 Right on Ralston Avenue at stop sign.

Hillsborough is a stately community tucked away in the hills of the San Francisco Peninsula. You may never be able to afford the rent here, but for a modest investment in time and energy you can enjoy this beautiful town by bicycle without even making a deposit.

A brief but grand tour of Hillsborough's estates begins in downtown San Mateo. Start near Talbot's, a well-known bicycle store and hobby shop on the corner of South B Street and Fifth. Phone (415) 342-0267. Ride west on Fifth. In a couple of blocks you'll come to Central Park, where there's a Japanese garden behind a high fence, next to the tennis courts.

Cross El Camino Real, and take a right at the next stop sign, on Dartmouth Road; there's a huge bay tree across the street. Dartmouth jogs left in one block. Cross West Third Avenue at a traffic light. Continue straight for a block to Arroyo Court, campsite of the first Gaspar de Portola expedition. The captain and his men stayed here in 1769, a few days after discovering San Francisco Bay.

Return to West Third Avenue and make your way to Crystal Springs Road. The narrow two-lane road winds gently uphill through a canyon that was carved out by San Mateo Creek. Polhemus Road, the last junction before Skyline, is named for Charles Polhemus, the director of the Southern Pacific Railroad in the 1860s.

During the climb to Skyline Boulevard, you'll ride under four massive concrete pillars supporting Interstate 280's Doran Bridge. Crystal Springs Dam is visible straight ahead. When completed in 1887, it was the largest concrete dam in the world. The dam withstood the 1906 earthquake undamaged.

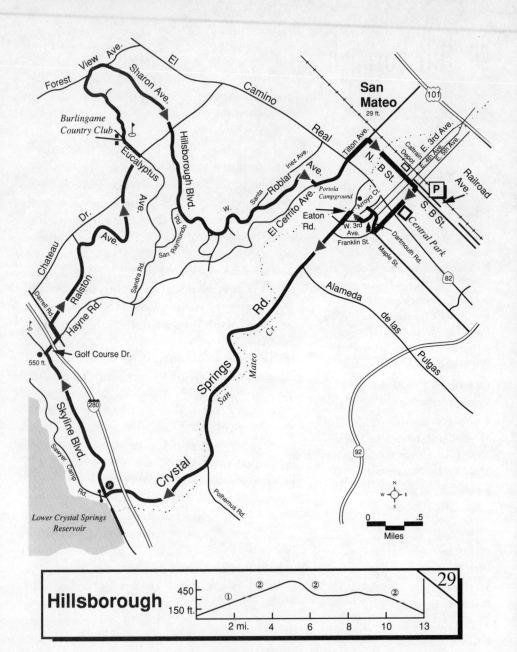

Forest View Ave.
El Camino Real
Sharon Ave.
Burlingame Country Club
Eucalyptus Ave.
Hillsborough Blvd.
W.
Santa
Roblar
Inez Ave.
Ave.
El Cerrito Ave.
Chateau Dr.
San Raymundo Rd.
Sandra Rd.
Ralston Ave.
Darrell Rd.
Hayne Rd.
Golf Course Dr.
550 ft.
Skyline Blvd.
280
Sawyer Camp Rd.
Lower Crystal Springs Reservoir
Crystal
Springs
Rd.
San Mateo
Cr.
Polhemus Rd.

San Mateo
29 ft.
Tilton Ave.
Caltrain Depot
N. B St.
Portola Campground
Arroyo Ct.
Eaton Rd.
W. 3rd Ave.
Franklin St.
S. B St.
Central Park
Dartmouth Rd.
Maple St.
Alameda
de las
Pulgas
E. 3rd Ave.
E. 4th Ave.
E. 5th Ave.
Railroad Ave.
P
101
82
92

N
W   E
S

0   .5
Miles

Hillsborough

450
150 ft.

① ② ② ②

2 mi.   4   6   8   10   13

29

7.5 Right on Chateau Drive at stop sign.

7.8 Left on Eucalyptus Avenue at stop sign. 7.9 Keep right at junction.

8.6 Right on Forest View Avenue at stop sign.

8.9 Right on Sharon Avenue. 9.1 Sharon Avenue becomes Hillsborough Boulevard.

10.4 Left on West Santa Inez Avenue. 10.7 Keep left at junction.

10.9 Bear right onto Roblar Avenue.

11.4 Left onto El Cerrito Avenue at stop sign. Becomes Tilton Avenue.

12.0 Right on North B Street.

12.5 End ride at Fifth and B.

Turn right at Skyline Boulevard, or you can extend the ride by riding straight on Sawyer Camp Road, behind the gate (see Casual Rides).

Climb on Skyline for 1.3 miles, turn right on Golf Course Drive, which becomes Hayne Road and ride under Interstate 280. Descend Ralston Avenue and turn left to ride past the exclusive Burlingame Country Club and golf course. President Teddy Roosevelt visited the club while campaigning in 1903. Founded in 1892 (at a different site) by San Francisco socialites, the club attracts the Peninsula's rich and famous. The road through the golf course is bordered by imposing white eucalyptus. Stay on Eucalyptus until Forest View Avenue, where there's an equally impressive stand of cypress lining the road.

Forest View winds around the golf course and heads south, becoming Sharon Avenue and then Hillsborough Boulevard. Sharon Avenue is named for Sen. William Sharon of Nevada, one of the early town builders on the Peninsula. There's a short, steep climb before you begin descending. You'll find some of the oldest and grandest of the Hillsborough estates at the bottom of the hill.

Hillsborough was incorporated in 1910. To maintain its privacy, the town annexed 8 square miles, all the way to Crystal Springs Dam, and does not permit business. Another contributor to privacy is the confusing street layout. Pay close attention to the roads, or you might wind up in Half Moon Bay.

30 Old La Honda Road

Distance: 39 miles
Terrain: Hilly
Traffic: Light to moderate

Mileage Log

0.0 Start mileage at Woodside School on Highway 84, 0.2 miles west of Cañada Road intersection. Ride east on Highway 84.

0.2 Right on Mountain Home Road at four-way stop. 0.6 Manzanita Road on left.

2.2 Left on Portola Road at stop sign.

2.4 Right at stop sign, staying on Portola Road.

2.8 Right on Old La Honda Road. Begin 3.4-mile climb. 6.2 Skyline Boulevard. Cross road and continue on Old La Honda Road. Begin descent.

8.8 Left on Highway 84 at stop sign. Stop, look, and listen before crossing at blind corner. 12.0 La Honda. Grocery store and restaurant on right in shopping center.

12.7 Left on Pescadero Road.

13.8 Continue straight onto Alpine Road in the redwoods. (Pescadero Road veers right.) 5.6-mile climb begins in 1 mile. 17.5 Entrance to honor camp and Pescadero Creek Park on right.

17.9 Left at stop sign. Right goes to Portola State Park. 21.3 Skyline Boulevard. Cross and continue on Page Mill Road. 22.0 Alpine Road

It may be narrow, steep, and bumpy, but Old La Honda Road draws bicyclists from all over San Mateo County. The road appeals to cyclists because it offers a traffic-free, scenic route to Skyline Boulevard from Portola Valley. The climb to Skyline Boulevard is steeper than on Highway 84 to the northwest, but 84 has a lot of traffic.

Many bicyclists start their rides in Woodside, a forested community known for its stately mansions and horse ranches. The town dates back to the mid-1800s, when logging was the main industry. The town's stores and hotels served wagon masters carrying logs to the port of Redwood City. Today's roads through Woodside carry cars, bicycles, and equestrians on busy weekends.

Cycling is so popular here that bicyclists outnumber cars on most weekends. With so many cars and bicycles using narrow roads, Woodside motorists and San Mateo County sheriffs have little patience for law-breaking cyclists. Ride carefully, and obey all traffic laws.

Old La Honda Road is one of the oldest logging roads in the area. It was extended to La Honda in 1876 and, like many early roads in the Coast Range, became a toll road—the Redwood City and Pescadero Turnpike.

Leave Woodside and ride south on Mountain Home Road, where you'll pass palatial estates hidden behind tan oak, eucalyptus, scotch broom, and redwoods. The road was built in 1872 to link Woodside with the town of Searsville. In the late 1880s, the town was abandoned and covered by water with the damming of San Francisquito Creek. Portola Road cuts across the reservoir's marshy backwaters.

Some historical landmarks are located at the beginning of Old La Honda Road. Preston Road,

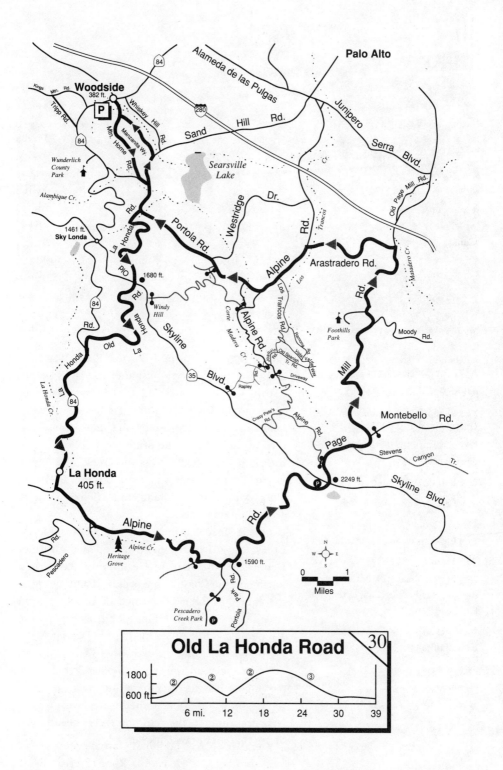

Palo Alto

84

Alameda de las Pulgas

Kings Mtn. Rd.

Woodside
382 ft.

P

Tripp Rd.

84

Whiskey Hill Rd.

Manzanita Wy.

Mtn. Home Rd.

Sand Hill Rd.

280

Junipero Serra Blvd.

Wunderlich County Park

Old Page Mill Rd.

Alambique Cr.

Searsville Lake

Westridge Dr.

La Honda Rd.

Portola Rd.

Alpine Rd.

Cr.

Los Trancos Cr.

1461 ft.
Sky Londa

Arastradero Rd.

Old La Honda Rd.

1680 ft.

Windy Hill

Corte Madera Cr.

Alpine Rd.

Los Trancos Rd.

Foothills Park

Page Mill Rd.

Moody Rd.

84

Old La Honda Rd.

Skyline

35

Blvd.

Rapley

Rd.

Los Trancos Tr. Rd.

Old Spanish Tr.

Driveway

Yerba Buena Way

Montebello Rd.

84

La Honda Cr.

Crazy Pete's Rd.

Alpine Rd.

Stevens Canyon Tr.

La Honda Rd.

La Honda
405 ft.

P

2249 ft.

Skyline Blvd.

Alpine

Rd.

Alpine Cr.

Heritage Grove

1590 ft.

N
W   E
S

0   1
Miles

Pescadero

Portola Park Rd.

Pescadero Creek Park

P

Old La Honda Road

30

1800

600 ft

②   ②   ②   ③

6 mi.   12   18   24   30   39

junction on left, behind green gate. Dirt road for 2.6 miles connects with paved Alpine Road.

27.1 Keep left at junction with Moody Road. 27.3 Entrance to Foothills Park. Drinking fountain outside gate.

29.6 Left on Arastradero Road.

31.6 Left on Alpine Road at stop sign.

32.8 Right on Portola Road at stop sign.

36.1 Portola Road on left. Continue straight. Road name changes to Sand Hill Road, unmarked.

36.8 Left on Manzanita Way near bottom of hill.

38.1 Right on Mountain Home Road at stop sign.

38.5 Left on Highway 84 at stop sign.

38.7 End of ride at Woodside School.

on the right, was formerly Portola Road. Watch for a stairway on your right just after you cross Dennis Martin Creek. It once led to a house owned by spice mogul August Schilling. He owned a lavishly landscaped 300-acre estate; the main house was torn down in 1953. The original guest house is on the right, before you cross the creek. Millionaire Edgar Preston built the mansion in the 1870s, along with a pond, hiking trails, flower gardens, and other amenities.

At the first hairpin, crossing Dennis Martin Creek, the driveway straight ahead is the former Dennis Martin Road, where some of the earliest logging in the Coast Range occurred. On the right, the trail that follows a branch of Dennis Martin Creek goes to the Schilling pond, owned by the Midpeninsula Regional Open Space District.

About 2 miles into the climb there's a steep right bend in the road where, in the stagecoach days, passengers had to disembark and walk—or push the wagon—until they reached more level ground. Near the summit, the redwood forest becomes so dense that it's always dark here.

Left: *Alpine Road leads to the heart of redwood country near the Pacific Ocean.*

Above: *Old La Honda Road was built in the mid-1800s for hauling redwood logs to the port of Redwood City.*

Cross Skyline Boulevard, called "Wonder Way" when it was conceived in 1917. The road, built from 1920 to 1929, extends 47 miles south from San Francisco. Skyline was widened and given its present alignment in the 1950s and 1960s.

Begin a descent on Old La Honda Road, which was paved for the first time in 1987. Turn left on Highway 84 at the stop sign, where there's a blind corner. Listen carefully for cars coming up the hill. Hot weekends bring out sun worshipers, who occasionally clog the wide two-lane highway. The descent into the town of La Honda is usually marked by a sudden and dramatic drop in temperature as you enter the redwoods.

Turn left on Pescadero Road after riding through La Honda, and continue straight onto Alpine Road at the bridge over Alpine Creek. Shortly you'll pass a Heritage Grove, which was saved from logging in the late 1960s and added to Sam McDonald County Park. The redwoods marked for cutting still have their blue paint.

Alpine Road climbs like a staircase, with steep sections between 8 and 10 percent. You'll have impressive views of the Pacific Coast, the Coast Range, and Mindego Hill to the north.

Cross Skyline Boulevard at the summit, and proceed on Page Mill Road. Parts of Page Mill were built by William Page, a gold miner who turned woodsman. He built the road in 1866 to get to his mill, located in Portola State Park. At the time it was built, the road was called the Mayfield and Pescadero Road. Mill was interested in the most direct route, and damn the horses. Some grades rise as steeply as 17 percent. Passengers taking the stagecoach to Pescadero must have had a thrilling journey.

Page Mill's steepest section begins midway down, at a hairpin, Shotgun Bend, so-called because it used to be a popular shooting area. Turn left on Arastradero Road at the bottom of Page Mill, and return to Woodside through Portola Valley.

31 Pescadero Road

Distance: 28 miles
Terrain: Several moderate hills
Traffic: Light

Mileage Log

0.0 Start mileage at the intersection of Stage Road and Pescadero Road in Pescadero. Ride north on Stage Road. 0.1 North Street on right. 2.4 Begin first 1-mile climb on Stage Road. 4.5 Begin final 0.8-mile climb on Stage Road.

7.1 Right on La Honda Road, Highway 84, at stop sign. Restrooms across the road at San Gregorio General Store.

14.6 Right on Pescadero Road at green sign to Sam McDonald Park.

15.7 Keep right on Pescadero Road at Alpine Road junction. Begin 1.6-mile climb. 16.3 Sam McDonald County Park entrance. Restrooms and water. 17.3 Haskins Hill summit. 19.9 Entrance to Memorial Park. Restrooms and water. 21.3 Loma Mar Store. Portable toilet, water, food. 25.1 "Pumpkin Tree" on right in front of house and next to hedge. 25.8 Butano Cutoff on left. 26.3 Phipps Ranch on left.

26.5 Right on North Street.

27.4 Left on Stage Road at stop sign.

27.5 End of ride in Pescadero.

Remote canyons, pristine streams, and quiet farm towns in the southwest corner of San Mateo County give bicyclists plenty to see and enjoy here. Your ride starts in the coastal town of Pescadero and makes a loop on Stage Road, Highway 84, and Pescadero Road.

Pescadero looks a lot like it did a century ago. Alan Hynding, in his book *From Frontier to Suburb,* compared it to a New England community. Its 400 residents lived quiet, pastoral lives. A thriving lumber industry upstream on Pescadero Creek helped maintain the town's four stores, livery stables, and two hotels. Later, dairy farming became the town's mainstay.

Head north on Stage Road, the old coast highway. You'll ride through a wide, long valley, with eucalyptus trees lining the road and horses grazing in meadows. You may hear the cry of a peacock at Willowside Farm at the end of a row of eucalyptus.

Begin a short, easy climb where the road circles a hayfield. In the middle of the field there's a metal shed used for testing electronic equipment. The location was chosen for its isolation from radio transmissions. At the summit, you'll have a panorama of Stage Road as it winds down to Pomponio Creek and then up the next ridge. You'll have two descents before reaching San Gregorio. After crossing San Gregorio Creek, you can see the old stagecoach stop on the left at Highway 84. The San Gregorio General Store across the highway stays open seven days a week.

Turn right on La Honda Road, Highway 84, and ride up a wide agricultural valley. Typically you'll have a tailwind, but headwinds farther inland. The road climbs gradually as it follows San Gregorio Creek.

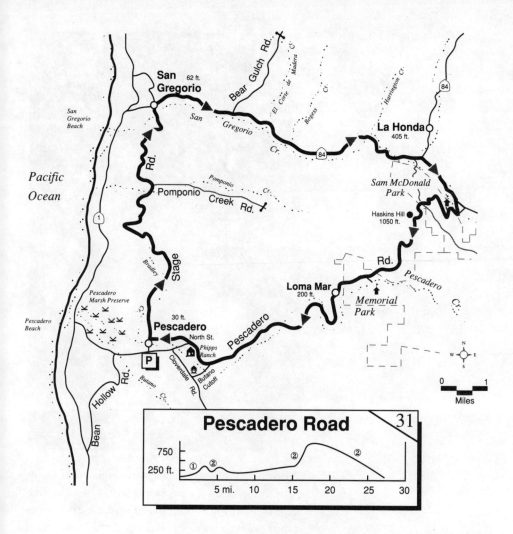

Pescadero Road 31

About a quarter-mile from where you'll turn right, look for a yellow log cabin on the right. Ken Kesey, author of *One Flew Over the Cuckoo's Nest*, lived here in the 1960s. His wild parties with Timothy Leary attracted national attention, not to mention the county sheriffs.

Turn right onto Pescadero Road at the green road sign for Sam McDonald County Park. You'll pass the park headquarters (water and restrooms here) on the right in a half-mile. Pescadero Road was built by the county in 1876.

At the top of Haskins Hill you can see Butano Ridge to the south. Now begin a long, sweeping

Stage Road, formerly the coast highway,
sees little traffic.

descent to Memorial Park and Loma Mar. Don't miss a stop at the Loma Mar store. It has a lounge with a television, pool table, fireplace, and tables outside where you can soak up the sun on warm days. From Loma Mar, the road twists and turns as it follows Pescadero Creek through the redwoods. If you're riding here in autumn, watch for an apple tree with small pumpkins hanging from it, on the right in front of a house. The road leaves the canyon and passes through farmland, with Pescadero High School on the left. It's flat the rest of the way into town.

Road Rides

32 Portola Valley

Distance: 16 miles
Terrain: Gently rolling hills
Traffic: Moderate

Mileage Log

0.0 Start mileage on Stanford University campus next to Stanford stadium on Galvez Street. There's plenty of parking available next to Angel Field at Eucalyptus Drive. Ride west on Galvez Street.

0.1 Left on Campus Drive East at stop sign.

1.7 Right on Junipero Serra Boulevard at traffic light. 2.1 Campus Drive West intersection.

2.7 Left on Alpine Road at traffic light. 5.7 Arastradero Road intersection. Alpine Inn on left.

6.9 Right on Portola Road at stop sign. 9.7 Old La Honda Road intersection.

10.3 Keep right at junction. Begin Sand Hill Road. Portola Road goes left. 10.9 Manzanita Way intersection. 11.0 Whiskey Hill Road intersection. Begin climb. 11.7 Top of hill. 12.4 Interstate 280. 14.0 Santa Cruz Avenue intersection.

14.2 Right onto recreation path immediately after crossing San Francisquito Creek bridge.

14.7 Left on Campus Drive West at stop sign.

16.0 Left on Galvez Street. End of ride.

"The Loop," as it's known to local cyclists, draws throngs of fair-weather riders clad in colorful jerseys on Sunday mornings. It's the place to see and be seen. Stanford stadium is a convenient landmark to start the ride. Ride through the campus to Alpine Road. The Costanoan Indians were the first to use the route taken by Alpine Road. Antonio Buelna, the first recorded settler in Portola Valley in 1839, drove horse and wagon on the road when it was called Old Spanish Trail. Today Alpine Road has a wide shoulder and a recreation path on the south side, but it's narrow and bumpy and popular with walkers and runners. Yield at driveways and intersections, if you ride the path.

Alpine Road climbs gradually, passing meadows, oak-covered hills, homes, a country club, and baseball and soccer fields. Coyote, fox, and bobcats are occasionally seen from the road. Alpine Inn, the oldest road tavern in California (founded 1840), is located at the intersection of Arastradero Road and Alpine.

Turn right onto Portola Road at the stop sign, where there's a convenience store, a gas station, and a small shopping center. Portola Valley's town center is a mile and a half from Portola and Alpine roads. City council meetings are held in a school built over the San Andreas Fault, which formed the valley. Perhaps that's why the town council often "splits" on important issues.

Andrew Hallidie, inventor of the cable car, lived in Portola Valley in the 1880s. He built an experimental tramway from the valley floor into the mountains, across the road from what is now the shopping center.

You'll have a gradual downhill as you leave town. In a curve near the bottom of the hill, you'll pass

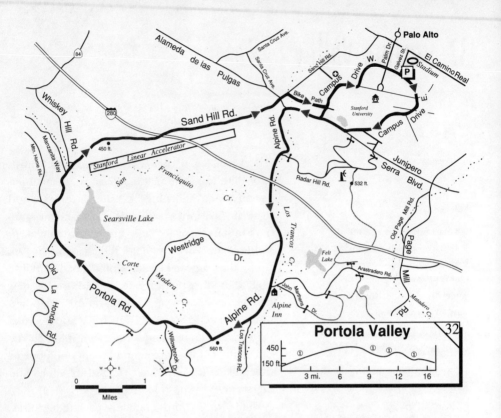

Old La Honda Road. Then Portola Road crosses a marshy inlet of Searsville reservoir. In the 1860s, Searsville was located nearby. The town grew on the strength of the logging industry and a short-lived silver "strike." But in 1879 the federal court ordered the town's residents to relocate and make way for the reservoir, which was built in 1891. The drinking water was intended for San Francisco, but it was never used for that purpose. Today the reservoir and the land around it comprise the Stanford Jasper Ridge preserve.

Return on Sand Hill Road, one of the oldest roads in San Mateo County. It was used as early as the 1790s by Spanish settlers harvesting timber for the Bay Area's missions. At the top of the climb on Sand Hill, you'll have a grand view of the bay and the East Bay hills. Descend to Santa Cruz Avenue and continue straight. Cross San Francisquito Creek and immediately turn right on a bike path that takes you to Campus Drive West. Turn left and return to the stadium.

33 San Bruno Mountain

Distance: 14 miles
Terrain: Two moderate hills
Traffic: Light to moderate

Mileage Log

0.0 Start mileage at entrance to San Bruno Mountain State and County Park and Guadalupe Canyon Parkway. Left from parking lot onto Guadalupe Canyon Parkway.

2.1 Right on Bayshore Boulevard at traffic light.

4.4 Right on Hillside Boulevard extension.

8.6 Right on Guadalupe Canyon Road at traffic light.

10.5 Right at gate, directly across from entrance to San Bruno Mountain Park entrance. Start climbing Radio Road. 12.0 Summit parking lot. Return same way.

13.5 Keep right and ride through parking lot and Guadalupe Canyon Road underpass.

13.7 Ride ends at main parking lot.

With barren slopes, San Bruno Mountain rises like a pyramid on the narrow San Francisco Peninsula. Although only a few trees grow on the mountain, the drab exterior reveals fragile beauty when seen up close by bicycle. Thanks to the efforts of conservationists, much of the mountain has been preserved as open space. You can ride to the summit to be rewarded with spectacular views of San Francisco.

On your ride you'll see numerous lush glens, which support the endangered San Bruno Elfin and Callippe Silverspot butterflies, and 14 species of rare or endangered plants. A prolonged battle between developers and environmentalists ultimately resulted in a 2,326-acre park. The Save San Bruno Mountain citizen's group is devoted to preserving open space. In 1978, San Mateo County and the state purchased 1,500 acres, with more acreage donated. The mountain has 12 miles of hiking trails and a paved road to the summit, where you'll find TV transmission towers.

The tour starts from the park's main staging area. You'll begin with a brisk descent to the bay and a ride on Old Bayshore Boulevard. The boulevard takes you past the secluded town of Brisbane. Old Bayshore was the main highway along the Peninsula until the mid-1960s, when Highway 101 was opened.

Turn right on the new Hillside Boulevard extension, and ride up a short, steep hill. As you round the western side of the mountain, you'll pass a hodgepodge of industrial parks, cemeteries, and commercial flower gardens in the town of Colma. Near Olivet Memorial Park, on the north side of Hillside, there's even a pet cemetery. Colma was a thriving agricultural town in the late 1800s. In the

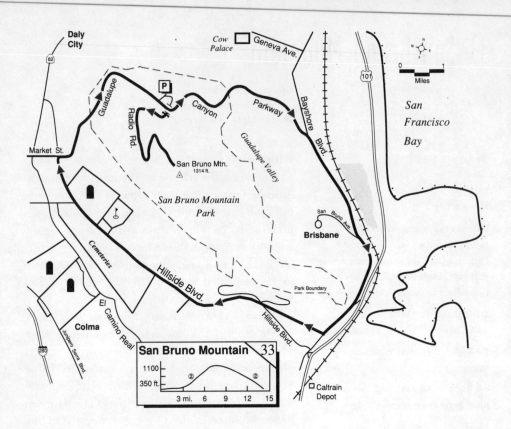

Daly
City

Cow
Palace   Geneva Ave.

101

N

0   1

Miles

Guadalupe

Radio Rd.

P

Canyon

Parkway

Bayshore Blvd.

San
Francisco
Bay

Market St.

San Bruno Mtn.
△ 1314 ft.

Guadalupe Valley

San Bruno Mountain
Park

San
Bruno Ave

Brisbane

Cemeteries

Hillside Blvd.

Park Boundary

Hillside Blvd.

El Camino Real

Colma

280

Junipero Serra Blvd

San Bruno Mountain   33

1100

350 ft.

②   ②

3 mi.   6   9   12   15

Caltrain
Depot

82

1890s the character of the land changed dramatically as farm plots were replaced by burial plots. Colma become forever linked with cemeteries in 1907 when San Francisco banned burials within its city limits and turned to Colma for burial space. The Catholic Holy Cross Cemetery, founded in 1887, became the first of more than a dozen cemeteries. At least a million people are buried in Colma, including newspaper publisher William Randolph Hearst and lawman Wyatt Earp. Colma wasn't incorporated until 1941, with 500 living residents.

East Market Street, with its many small stores, becomes Guadalupe Canyon Parkway, beginning a gradual 1.8-mile climb to San Bruno Mountain Park. In the past, there has been a New Year's day San Bruno Mountain race, going from the base of the mountain to the summit.

Your ride finishes dramatically with a 1.4-mile climb to the summit on a road that's closed to cars. One day as I was riding up, I saw a fox saunter across the road, stop, and watch me as I rode by. At the summit, the Marin headlands and the Golden Gate Bridge fill the northern horizon like a picture postcard.

Admission to the parking area is $3 per car, free for bicycles. The park has picnic tables, restrooms, and a drinking fountain.

It can be cold and windy on the mountain, so dress appropriately. In contrast, during an inversion you may find the weather cold and hazy at the base of the mountain but warm and sunny on top. For more information contact San Mateo County Parks Department; call (415) 363-4020.

34 San Francisco

Distance: 28 miles
Terrain: Mostly flat; a few gentle hills
Traffic: Light to moderate

Mileage Log

0.0 Start mileage at Embarcadero and Folsom. Ride north on Embarcadero. 0.3 Ferry Building. 1.8 Fisherman's Wharf. 2.2 Dolphin South End Club and Maritime Museum. Road becomes walkway.

2.6 Left at concrete pier.

3.1 Right at Laguna then left on Marina recreation path. 4.0 Enter U.S. Army gate to Presidio.

4.4 Left on Halleck Street under Highway 101 causeway at stop sign.

4.6 Right on Lincoln Boulevard at stop sign. 6.1 Golden Gate Bridge parking lot entrance. 6.7 Lincoln Boulevard summit. Begin descent. Lincoln becomes El Camino del Mar at bottom of hill.

8.7 Left on Legion of Honor Drive. Legion of Honor art museum.

9.2 Right on Geary Boulevard at stop sign. Geary changes to Point Lobos Avenue as it turns south, then becomes Great Highway. 10.2 Cliff House restaurant on right. Keep clear of parked cars. 11.3 Take Great Highway bike lane or recreation path on left. 13.3 San Francisco Zoo on left.

14.1 Right on Skyline Boulevard at stop sign, or cross Skyline and pick up Lake Merced recreation path.

San Francisco is known for its steep streets and traffic congestion, but if you'll follow my route you can avoid both obstacles and see the most beautiful sections of the city. The route loops counterclockwise to include such popular attractions as the Golden Gate Bridge, Fisherman's Wharf, the Pacific Ocean, Golden Gate Park, and downtown. Do this ride on a Sunday when traffic is light. After your ride you may want to visit the Embarcadero Center, where you'll be dazzled by the Hyatt Regency Hotel's free-standing glass elevators.

The tour starts at the intersection of Folsom and Embarcadero next to the Bay Bridge. And no, there isn't any free parking here either. You can take your bicycle into the city on BART or the peninsula train, or use one of the many pay parking lots. Ride north past numbered rows of piers that jut from the flat, wide Embarcadero. In 1987 a maze of railroad tracks was paved over, making cycling safer here. The ride along the Embarcadero is more scenic with the removal of the Embarcadero overpass, which was shaken into submission in the 1989 temblor and torn down in 1991. The historic Ferry Building and World Trade Center, built in 1898, are no longer hidden by the freeway. The Ferry Building was one of a handful of buildings along the waterfront that survived the 1906 earthquake and fire. The Golden Gate Ferry and Red & White Fleet, with service to Sausalito, Tiburon, Oakland, and Vallejo, serve commuters and tourists from here.

After another mile on the Embarcadero, you'll reach Fisherman's Wharf at Pier 45. A small fishing fleet still docks here, next to the pier's tourist shops. Harbor cruises and Alcatraz Island tours leave from Pier 45.

Road Rides

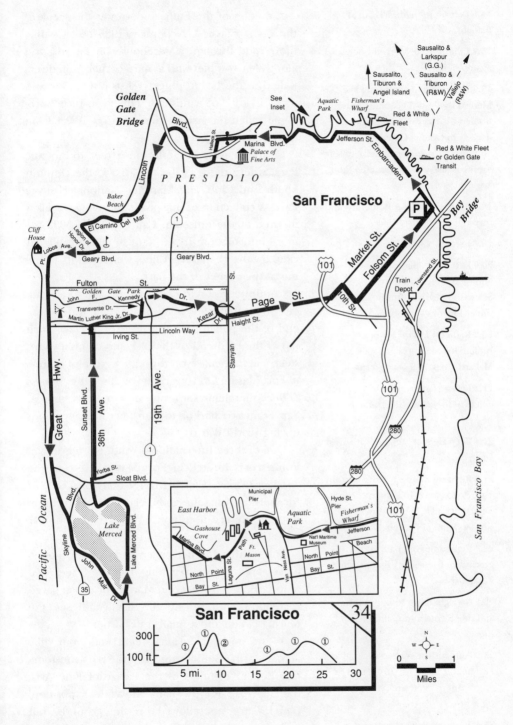

Golden
Gate
Bridge

Blvd.

Hallock St.

See Inset

Aquatic
Park

Fisherman's
Wharf

Red & White
Fleet

Sausalito &
Larkspur
(G.G.)

Sausalito,
Tiburon &
Angel Island

Sausalito &
Tiburon
(R&W)

Vallejo
(R&W)

Marina Blvd.

Palace of
Fine Arts

Jefferson St.

Embarcadero

Red & White Fleet
or Golden Gate
Transit

P R E S I D I O

San Francisco

Baker
Beach

Lincoln

Cliff
House

El Camino Del Mar

Legion of
Honor Dr.

Pt. Lobos Ave.

Geary Blvd.

Geary Blvd.

101

Market St.

Folsom St.

P

Bay
Bridge

Townsend St.

Fulton   St.

Golden Gate Park

John   F.   Kennedy

Dr.

Page   St.

Train
Depot

Transverse Dr.

Martin Luther King Jr. Dr.

Kezar
Dr.

Haight St.

Stanyan

St.

10th St.

101

Lincoln Way

Irving St.

Great

Hwy.

Sunset Blvd.

36th   Ave.

19th   Ave.

1

280

101

280

Yorba St.

Sloat Blvd.

Skyline

Blvd.

Lake
Merced

John   Muir   Dr.

Lake Merced Blvd.

35

Pacific

Ocean

San Francisco Bay

Municipal
Pier

East Harbor

Gashouse
Cove

Marina Blvd.

Aquatic
Park

Hyde St.
Pier
Fisherman's
Wharf

Nat'l Maritime
Museum

Jefferson

Ft.
Mason

Path

Laguna St.

Van Ness Ave.

North   Point

North   Point

Beach

Bay   St.

Bay   St.

San Francisco

34

300

100 ft.

① ① ② ① ① ①

5 mi.   10   15   20   25   30

N
W   E
S

0   1

Miles

14.6 Left on John Muir Drive at traffic light.

15.7 Left on Lake Merced Boulevard at stop sign.

17.7 Keep right at junction. Lake Merced Boulevard becomes Sunset Boulevard. You can take Sunset all the way to Golden Gate Park or use 36th Avenue, which parallels Sunset. Traffic is heavy on Sunset after 9:00 A.M.

18.0 Ride under Sloat Boulevard and turn right on Yorba Street.

18.1 Left on 36th Avenue.

20.0 Left on Irving Street at stop sign and then immediately turn right on Sunset Boulevard at traffic light. Ride under Lincoln Way bridge.

20.2 Right on Martin Luther King Junior Drive at stop sign. 20.8 Mallard Lake. 20.9 Giant ferns.

21.2 Left on Transverse Drive. A difficult turn to make when traffic is heavy.

21.4 Keep right at junction with West Drive.

21.6 Right on Kennedy Drive at stop sign. Road closed to auto traffic every Sunday. 22.5 De Young Museum. 22.8 Conservatory of Flowers.

22.9 Right on paved path (note green bike route sign) that parallels Kezar Drive.

23.1 Go right down hill, turn left, and ride through tunnel under Kezar.

23.2 Path ends at crosswalk signal at Haight and Stanyan. Turn left here onto Stanyan. Stanyan Cyclery on right.

23.3. Right on Page Street.

A section of the Embarcadero was the scene of the Coors Classic bicycle race (1985–86). Competitors rode through a warehouse on Pier 45 and along a narrow pier with a sharp corner. Skin divers waited in the bay to pluck cyclists out of the cold water in case of a mishap. The stage race's prologue called for a steep climb to Coit Tower from the Embarcadero.

Continue west on Jefferson Street to Aquatic Park, where there's a beach, a park, the Dolphin South End Club, and Maritime National Historic Park. A collection of one-of-a-kind sailing vessels is moored at the museum. Call (415) 556-3002 for more information. If you want to take a cable car ride, try the Hyde Street line, which has its terminus at the corner of the park.

Continue west and climb a short hill to a dead-end street that leads to Municipal Pier. Ride to the end of the pier for a better view of the bay. Turn left at the land end of the pier and climb a short, steep hill that takes you through a grove of cypress in Fort Mason. On your right you'll see the *Jeremiah O'Brien* merchant ship, one of hundreds built in San Francisco harbor to transport military goods during World War II.

One of three International Youth Hostels in San Francisco is located in Fort Mason, close to the *Jeremiah O'Brien*. Call (415) 788-5604 or 771-7277 for more information about economical overnight housing. Reservations are required at the popular hostel.

Ride a short distance on a paved path in an open grassy area before reaching Laguna Street and Marina Boulevard. Stay on Marina, or take a paved recreation path. Along the bay you'll see the Marina Green and a small-craft harbor.

At the end of Marina Green, walk your bike across Marina Boulevard to visit the red sandstone-like Roman columns of the Palace of Fine Arts, built in 1915 for the Panama-Pacific Exposition. Bicycles are not allowed on the grounds, but you can park your bike and take a stroll on a path around a peaceful lagoon. The science

The Palace of Fine Arts was built in 1915 for the Panama-Pacific International Exposition commemorating completion of the Panama Canal.

25.1 Merge onto Market Street at traffic light.

25.3 Right on Tenth Street at traffic light.

25.7 Left on Folsom Avenue at traffic light.

27.5 Return to start.

Exploratorium is also located here. For more information about the Exploratorium, call (415) 563-3200.

Return to Marina Boulevard and ride through the Presidio, Sixth Army headquarters; the base will become part of the Golden Gate National Recreation Area in Fall 1994. The base is currently open to the public on weekends. One of the adobe buildings built by the first Spanish settlers in 1776 is located on the base near the intersection of Arguello Boulevard and Funston Avenue. The army museum can be found on Funston Avenue at Lincoln Boulevard. For more information, call (415) 921-8193.

There's a steady, gentle climb through the base under a canopy of cypress and eucalyptus. Before riding under Highway 101, turn right into a parking lot for views of Golden Gate Bridge.

A short distance beyond the Highway 101 overpass, you'll begin a long descent on Lincoln, which becomes El Camino del Mar. Mediterranean-style houses here have spectacular views of the Golden Gate Bridge and the Marin headlands.

Farther along, you'll ride through Lincoln Park Golf Course and Lincoln Park. Turn left at the Palace of the Legion of Honor art museum, which was closed by earthquake damage (reopens in 1994). This World War I memorial is patterned after the Palace of the Legion of Honor in Paris.

Descend past the golf course to Geary Boulevard, followed by a steep downhill to the Great Highway and The Esplanade along the Pacific Ocean.

As you pass the Cliff House restaurant, watch for cars backing out from parking spaces. The Cliff House, overlooking Seal Rock and the Pacific, was built in 1858 by Sam Brannan. The house was originally assembled from lumber salvaged off a wrecked schooner. The restaurant has burned and been rebuilt several times.

At the bottom of the hill, Golden Gate Park's Dutch windmills next to the highway turn slowly in the ocean breeze. A volunteer organization restored the windmills to their former glory.

There's a recreation path, completed in 1988, on the left side of the Great Highway, or you can ride along the highway's wide shoulder. The San Francisco Zoo is located on Sloat Boulevard near the Great Highway. After the zoo, the highway is— once again—torn up for construction of the city's massive sewage treatment plant. Continue south on the Great Highway up a short hill and descend to Skyline Boulevard. Cross the road and pick up the recreation path along Lake Merced, or turn right and then turn left onto John Muir Drive.

Lake Merced Boulevard has a narrow recreation path that sees heavy use. Continue north on Sunset Boulevard, ride under Sloat Boulevard, and then turn right on Yorba Street. Take an immediate left and ride to Golden Gate Park on 36th Avenue.

Golden Gate Park extends 3 miles inland from the ocean. John McLaren, a Scottish landscape gardener who was the park superintendent from 1887 to 1943, shaped sand dunes and scrub into an urban forest. There's a gradual mile climb to Transverse Drive. Kennedy Drive is closed to cars every Sunday, 6:00 A.M. to 5:00 P.M.

On Kennedy you'll see the de Young Museum and the white-glass Conservatory of Flowers near the end of Kennedy Drive. California millionaire James Lick had the entire building packed up in London and shipped to California.

Ride under the Kezar Drive walkway, cross Stanyan Street at a crosswalk, and pick up Page Street one block to the north. Stanyan Street Cyclery is located at 672 Stanyan between Haight and Page; phone (415) 221-7211. You'll see some of the city's famous Victorian-style houses on Page. Although Page has many stop signs, traffic is light, and the hills are manageable. It's mostly downhill to Market Street, the main street through downtown San Francisco. Ride on Market three blocks, turn right onto 10th Street (one way), and then left on Folsom. This straight, wide one-way street returns you to the Embarcadero.

35 Stanford and Los Altos Hills

Distance: 19 miles
Terrain: Moderate hills
Traffic: Light to moderate

Mileage Log

0.0 Start mileage at Angel Field (next to Stanford stadium) at intersection of Galvez Drive and Campus Drive East on Stanford University campus. Ride north on Campus Drive East.

0.3 Left on Palm Drive at stop sign. Keep right when road splits.

0.8 Left on Serra Street at stop sign. Inner Quadrangle located directly west of bus stop on Serra Street. Walk bike through Inner Quadrangle to visit Stanford's Memorial Church. Continue south on Serra past Hoover Institution tower and fountain.

1.3 Right on Campus Drive East at stop sign.

1.6 Left on Bowdoin Street at stop sign. Continue straight at stop sign on Stanford Avenue.

2.3 Left on California Avenue at stop sign.

2.4 Right on Hanover Street at stop sign. Cross Page Mill Road at traffic light.

3.0 Left on bike path next to Varian building. Continue south through Bol Park on path.

4.2 Right on Arastradero Road, crossing Foothill Expressway at traffic light.

4.8 Left on Fremont Road at stop sign.

Stanford University is world-renowned for its academic excellence and attractive campus, and it also has miles of paths well suited for a relaxing bike tour. Bicycling has been popular here since the university opened in 1891. There's even a racing team. On school days, the paths are crowded with students riding to class, but on the weekends they're usually empty.

There is one drawback to riding on the paths—puncture vine. The thorny plant grows next to the paths. The thorns cause more flat tires than all other causes of flats on campus combined. The vine is easily identified by its delicate yellow flowers and frilly green leaves. It spreads in a circle from a central root, growing flat on the ground. The only sure protection from the vine's thorny brown seeds is avoidance.

Start riding from Stanford stadium. The stadium has plenty of parking, except during home games (Saturdays) for football. From Campus Drive East, turn left on Palm Drive. The crowned road is bordered by mature palm trees. Straight ahead you'll see the center of campus or "quadrangle," where Stanford's Memorial Church is located. Jane Stanford had the church built in 1903 in memory of her husband, Leland. He was one of four founders of the transcontinental Central Pacific Railroad and president of the Southern Pacific Railroad. Stanford served as U.S. Senator from 1885 until his death in 1893.

The massive sandstone blocks used to make the university's buildings were shipped by rail from a quarry in south San Jose. The stone buildings didn't hold up well in the 1906 earthquake—especially the church—so many buildings have been reinforced. The church was closed in 1989 after the Loma Prieta earthquake, but reopened in 1992.

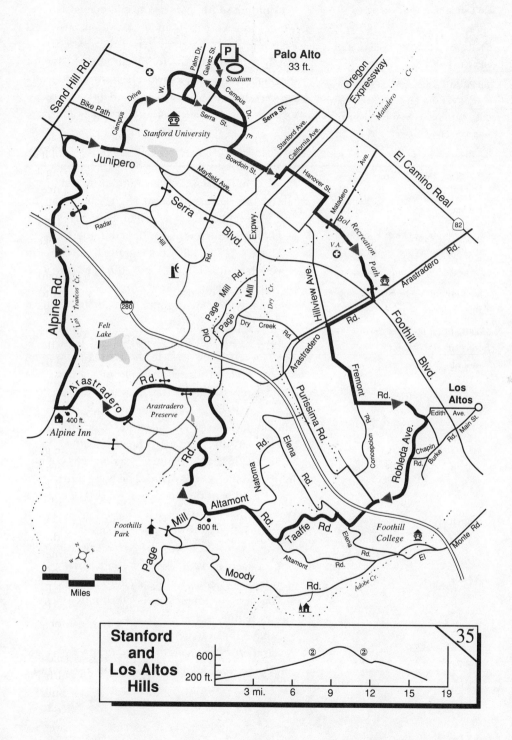

Palo Alto
33 ft.

Stadium

Stanford University

Sand Hill Rd.

Bike Path

Campus

Drive

W.

Palm Dr.

Galvez St.

Campus Dr.

Serra St.

Serra St.

Stanford Ave.

California Ave.

Oregon Expressway

Matadero Cr.

El Camino Real

82

Junipero

Mayfield Ave.

Serra Blvd.

Bowdoin St.

Expwy.

Hanover St.

Matadero Ave.

Bol Recreation Path

Arastradero Rd.

Radar

Hill Rd.

Page Mill Rd.

Page Mill Expwy.

Dry Cr.

Hillview Ave.

V.A.

Alpine Rd.

Los Trancos Cr.

280

Felt Lake

Page

Old Page Mill

Dry Creek Rd.

Arastradero Rd.

Rd.

Fremont Rd.

Foothill Blvd.

Los Altos

Arastradero

Rd.

Arastradero Preserve

Purissima Rd.

Concepcion Rd.

Robleda Ave.

Edith Ave.

Chapin Rd.

Burke Rd.

Main St.

400 ft.

Alpine Inn

Natoma Rd.

Elena Rd.

Altamont

Mill

Rd.

Taaffe Rd.

Elena Rd.

Foothill College

Monte Rd.

Foothills Park

800 ft.

Page

Moody

Rd.

Altamont Rd.

El

Adobe Cr.

0 _____ 1
Miles

N
W E
S

**Stanford
and
Los Altos
Hills**

600

200 ft.

3 mi.   6   9   12   15   19

35

5.8 Left at stop sign, staying on Fremont.

6.6 Right on Robleda Avenue. Begin climb to Page Mill Road.

7.8 Purissima Road. Turn right if you want to cut short ride and eliminate hills. Turn right on Arastradero at stop sign and retrace route.

8.0 Right on Elena Road at stop sign.

8.2 Left on Taaffe Road.

9.1 Right on Altamont Road at stop sign.

10.1 Right on Page Mill Road at stop sign. Begin descent.

12.0 Left on Arastradero Road.

14.0 Right on Alpine Road at stop sign.

17.0 Right on Junipero Serra Boulevard at traffic light.

17.4 Left on Campus Drive West.

19.0 Left on Galvez Street at stop sign. End ride.

Continue south, past the missile-shaped Hoover Tower, and leave campus on Bowdoin Street. At Page Mill Road the character of the ride changes briefly from residential to industrial park. Two of the Peninsula's best-known electronics and computer companies, Varian and Hewlett-Packard, are located at the corner of Hanover Street and Page Mill.

Locate the recreation path that goes behind Varian and into Bol Park, bordered by Matadero Creek. You'll pass a Veterans Administration hospital, on the right, and Gunn High School, on the left. The bike path is a former Southern Pacific right-of-way, which was abandoned in the 1950s.

There's a steady but gradual climb on Arastradero Road. Los Altos Hills, and the hills themselves, begin at Fremont Road. The rural community was incorporated in 1956 to guard against rampant growth.

Take Taaffe Road, named for the family that once owned 3,000 acres in the area. You'll see an apricot orchard along one side of a ridge. The climb steepens the last few hundred yards before Altamont Road. After some ups and downs on Altamont, turn right and descend Page Mill Road.

Turn left on Arastradero Road, which was built in the 1830s as a shortcut for wagon teams hauling lumber to the port of Alviso. The huge tree stumps on either side of the road are remnants of eucalyptus trees that burned in a 1985 fire. The fire swept over the hills, destroying several houses.

Arastradero Preserve, a 600-acre Palo Alto park that opened in 1987, is on the left. Hiking trails lead from Arastradero to a secluded pond. In the spring golden poppies and yellow mustard grass cover the hills.

Alpine Inn, at the intersection of Alpine and Arastradero roads, sells food and drink. Turn right on Alpine Road, and it's all downhill to Stanford.

36 Tunitas Creek Road

Distance: 37 miles
Terrain: Two long climbs
Traffic: Light

Mileage Log

0.0 Start mileage at Woodside Town Hall and school on Highway 84, 0.2 miles west of the Cañada Road intersection. Ride west on Highway 84, also called Woodside Road.

0.1 Right on Albion Avenue.

0.3 Left on Manuella Avenue.

0.9 Right on Kings Mountain Road at stop sign. 1.3 Woodside Store on left at Tripp Road. 2.8 Huddart Park entrance. 4.1 Road widens briefly.

5.7 Skyline Boulevard junction at stop sign. Cross Skyline and Kings Mountain Road becomes Tunitas Creek Road. 6.9 Star Hill Road on left. 7.9 Trailhead to Purisima Creek Road on right. 8.7 Shingle Mill Road on left. Private property. 10.4 Mitchell Creek Road on left. Private property. 11.3 Lobitos Creek Road on right. Dirt road to Highway 1.

13.0 Keep left. Lobitos Creek Cutoff on right. Paved road to Highway 1.

15.0 Left on Highway 1 at stop sign. 16.0 Old entrance to Star Hill Road on left.

16.6 Left on Stage Road.

17.7 Left on Highway 84 at stop sign and San Gregorio General Store. 19.8 Bear Gulch Road on left. Goes to Skyline Boulevard, crossing private property. 24.8 Ken Kesey house on

During the logging boom of the late 1800s, Tunitas Creek Road and Kings Mountain Road became the main routes for wagons carrying redwood logs to Santa Clara Valley. Today the roads are important to a small population of mountain residents and to cyclists who enjoy riding through the redwoods.

The ride starts in Woodside at the base of the Coast Range. The first mile takes a route that avoids Woodside Road. In the summer you can help yourself to blackberries growing along Albion Road. You'll need the energy because Kings Mountain Road has a 10-percent grade right after the Woodside Store museum, and averages 7 percent most of the way.

The store—built in 1854—is Woodside's oldest building. Tripp Road, where the store stands, is named for store owner Robert Tripp. He was also a dentist, saloon keeper, postmaster, and one of the original San Mateo County supervisors. His store thrived off trade with loggers and teamsters who were hauling logs to the ports of Redwood City and Alviso.

Kings Mountain Road climbs to Skyline Boulevard through redwoods, oaks, bay laurel, and tan oak. Notice that many road signs around these parts have bullet holes, put there by our best marksmen. But not the Huddart Park sign. Its big, bold yellow letters are made of thick steel plate. Midway up the narrow road there's a wide straightaway. In the mid-1960s the county replaced a wooden bridge and widened the road. Locals were not appreciative. Coincidentally, other parts of Kings Mountain Road went with little repair for the next 15 years.

Near Skyline Boulevard you'll pass the site of Summit Springs Hotel, where mountain men met

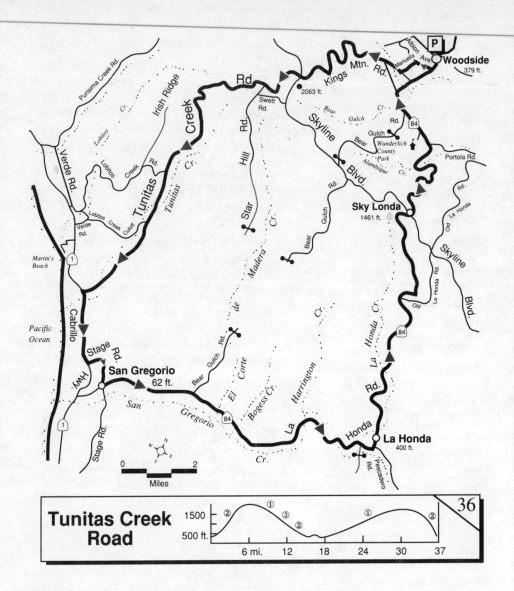

Tunitas Creek Road

36

mountain women to play a friendly game of checkers. The building has long since been torn down.

Tunitas Creek Road begins at Skyline and extends to the coast. It was called Froment's Road when built in 1868 by Eugene Froment, who used it for hauling logs from his sawmill at the Lobitos Creek Cutoff junction on Tunitas Creek. It was a toll road until the county bought it in 1884 for $3,000. The road was first paved in 1936.

There's a gradual descent for 2 miles, followed by steep hairpin curves; the road is often wet in the winter and on foggy summer mornings. Some of the old logging roads nearby include Purisima Creek, Star Hill, Swett, Richards, Shingle Mill, Grabtown, and Lobitos Creek. Star Hill is another toll road that went to the coast, but unfortunately it was abandoned by San Mateo County after they bought it. Purisima Creek Road, north of Tunitas Creek, can be reached by taking Grabtown Trail on the right (described in Mileage Log).

At Highway 1 you'll see flower farms. Turn left, cross Tunitas Creek, and begin a half-mile climb. Highway 1 has a wide shoulder most of the way to Stage Road, at the top of the hill.

Turn left on Stage Road and descend to San Gregorio. There's a gradual climb on Highway 84 to Skyline Boulevard and the village of Sky Londa; the steepest part comes a couple of miles above La Honda. From Sky Londa, descend Highway 84 to Woodside. Watch out for the first few curves; they can be wet and oily. Continue straight at the bottom of the hill, and it's only a couple of miles into town under the shade of eucalyptus.

37 Big Basin Redwoods State Park

Distance: 57 miles
Terrain: Hilly
Traffic: Light to moderate

Mileage Log

0.0 Start mileage at intersection of 4th Street and Highway 9 in downtown Saratoga. Parking available at Wildwood Park on 4th Street. Ride west on Highway 9. 0.5 Hakone Japanese Gardens on left. Road is steep into park. 1.5 Pierce Road junction on right. 3.0 Mariani Vineyards on left. 3.3 Dog City. 3.9 Redwood Gulch Road junction on right.

7.0 Skyline Boulevard junction at stop sign. Continue straight on Highway 9.

13.1 Right onto Highway 236 at junction. 16.2 Summit.

17.8 Straight on Highway 236 at China Grade junction. 18.9 Service Road on right at gate. 21.3 Big Basin Redwoods State Park headquarters on left, with restrooms and water. Food and drink 50 yards on right at store. 24.5 Summit. 28.0 Jamison Creek Road junction on right. Steep road.

30.6 Left at stop sign onto Highway 9 in Boulder Creek.

30.7 Right on Bear Creek Road immediately after crossing Boulder Creek Bridge. 35.1 Begin 4.7-mile climb. 39.5 David Bruce and Bear Creek wineries. 39.8 Summit.

Here's a route for cyclists who want to see the "big picture"—big redwoods, Big Basin Redwoods State Park, big climbs, and big descents. Start the ride in downtown Saratoga (founded 1855), gateway to the 7-mile climb to Saratoga Gap at Skyline Boulevard. The climb has a steady grade of about 6 percent.

Highway 9 follows Saratoga Creek for several miles. Just before crossing the creek you'll pass Congress Springs campground. This site attracted tourists in 1866 when someone decided to promote the creek's mineral springs as having curative powers. People from all over the world flocked here to drink and bathe. Farther up Highway 9, on the left, there's a driveway to Mariani Vineyards (formerly Congress Springs Vineyards), one of many small vineyards in the Santa Cruz Mountains. The winery was established in the 1890s by a French immigrant, Pierre Pourroy. The main building was erected in 1923.

There's a parking lot at Saratoga Gap, but no facilities. The Skyline to the Sea Trail starts near the southwest corner of the intersection and follows the old Saratoga Toll Road for several miles before crossing Highway 9 and continuing to Big Basin Redwoods State Park; phone (408) 338-6132. Bicycles are prohibited on the toll road.

Cross Skyline Boulevard and begin a 6-mile descent to Highway 236 junction at Waterman Gap. Highway 236, a lightly traveled, narrow, twisty road, climbs gradually through a canopy of tan oak, manzanita, and bay laurel. It was built in the early 1900s to make the park more accessible. Look west from China Grade junction, and you'll see the Eagle Rock formation looming over Big Basin.

P Saratoga
480 ft.

2634 ft.

Castle Rock
State Park

Mt. Bielawski
3000 ft.

Skyline

Blvd.

Old Haul Rd.

China Grade

236

Big Basin
Redwoods
State Park

China Grade

Lodge
Rd.

1000 ft.

Eagle Rock
2488 ft.

San Lorenzo River

Kings Creek

Kings

Bar

Rd.

Rd.

Cr.

Two Bar Cr.

Bear

Creek

Rd.

Two Bar

Bear Cr.

Sanborn Rd.

McKenzie
Reservoir

Black Rd.

Summit

Gist Rd.

Bear Creek Rd.

Rd.

2200 ft.

Loch Lomond
Reservoir

Summit Rd.

Summit Rd.

Upper E. Zayante Rd.

Empire Grade

Jamison
Creek Rd.

Boulder Cr.

Boulder
Creek
500 ft.

Alba Rd.

Glen Arbor Rd.

Ben
Lomond

Empire   Grade

Pine Flat Rd.

Ice Cream Grade

Martin Rd.

Bonny
Doon

Henry Cowell
Redwoods
State Park

Felton   Empire   Rd.

9

Quail Hollow Rd.

Lompico Rd.

E. Zayante Rd.

Zayante Cr.

Mt. Hermon Rd.

Felton

17

Big Basin Redwoods State Park   37

2400

800 ft.

②   ②   ②   ②

10 mi.   20   30   40   50   57

N
W   E
S

0   3
Miles

40.1 **Left** on Summit Road. 43.9 Black Road junction on right. Road widens and becomes Skyline Boulevard. 47.2 Summit at 3,000 feet. 47.7 Castle Rock State Park entrance. No facilities.

50.3 **Right** on Highway 9.

57.3 End of ride in Saratoga.

At park headquarters, you'll see impressive stands of redwoods. The park was founded in 1902 to protect the largest remaining concentration of old-growth redwoods in the Santa Cruz Mountains. About 3,500 acres of the park's 16,000 acres contain redwoods dating back to the Crusades. Fifty yards north of park headquarters there's a food store, snack bar, and museum.

Continue south on Highway 236, climb out of the basin, and then descend 5 miles to Boulder Creek, a former logging town that retains its rustic charm. Turn left onto Highway 9 (grocery corner at the junction), cross Boulder Creek, and immediately turn right on Bear Creek Road. There's a gradual climb for several miles as the road follows Bear Creek, but then it takes on a decidedly steeper slope of about 9 percent for a couple of miles. Bear Creek Road was built in 1875 as a toll road. Santa Cruz County bought the road in 1890 for $500.

Turn left on Summit Road and begin a stair-step climb to Black Road. The road offers views of the San Lorenzo River basin and Los Gatos. The narrow Summit Road becomes Skyline Boulevard at Black Road, where the road widens. The climbing isn't over until Mt. Bielawski at about 3,000 feet. Shortly after the summit, you'll pass the entrance to Castle Rock State Park, a popular hiking and climbing destination. It's all downhill the last 9 miles into Saratoga.

38 Corralitos and Mt. Madonna

Distance: 74 miles
Terrain: Hilly
Traffic: Light to moderate

Mileage Log

0.0 Start mileage on East Main Street in downtown Los Gatos at the Highway 17 overpass next to the Los Gatos Creek Trail. Ride east on East Main Street. Becomes Los Gatos Boulevard.

0.9 Right on Kennedy Road at traffic light. 3.3 Summit.

4.2 Right on Shannon Road at stop sign.

4.9 Left on Hicks Road at stop sign.

5.9 Right on Camden Avenue at traffic light. 6.6 Summit.

8.3 Right on Almaden Expressway at traffic light.

10.0 Right on Almaden Road at traffic light.

10.6 Left on McKean Road.

10.9 Right on McKean Road at stop sign. Becomes Uvas Road.

19.4 Keep right on Uvas Road at Oak Glen Avenue junction.

27.1 Right on Watsonville Road at stop sign.

29.5 Right on Redwood Retreat Road.

32.6 Left on Mt. Madonna Road. Road turns to dirt in 2 miles. Steep grade.

38.3 Keep left on Mt. Madonna Road at summit; begin descent.

Although San Jose's urban congestion continues its inexorable spread into the southern reaches of Santa Clara County, there is still plenty of open countryside to be enjoyed here by bicycle. On this ride you'll see sprawling ranches, secluded parks, and redwood canyons. There is one difficult section of the ride in Mt. Madonna County Park that will test your climbing skills. If you do this ride in the other direction, headwinds at the end of the ride will test your endurance.

Start in downtown Los Gatos and ride southeast. The first climb on Kennedy Road will be a warmup to prepare you for the long stretch of rolling hills in the countryside on McKean Road and Uvas Road. Watch carefully for the left turn onto McKean Road from Almaden Road.

McKean and Uvas roll along through oak-covered hills. Having ridden past sprawling developments to get here, open countryside comes as a pleasant change. But Redwood Retreat Road defines the word *remote*. You'll enjoy a trickling stream and the shade of oak trees in relative isolation.

Mt. Madonna Road was the only road over the hills to Watsonville until Hecker Pass Highway was built to replace it. Mt. Madonna Road turns to dirt and gets steeper and steeper, but fortunately you'll have the cool shade of redwoods and relative solitude in which to make the assault. At the summit and junction you'll see one of the larger and more bizarre-looking redwoods in the area. The tree's massive trunk makes a good place to stop and rest before the descent on paved Mt. Madonna Road, which drops you into an agricultural valley with endless acres of fruit orchards. The ride is best enjoyed in the spring when the fruit trees are blossoming.

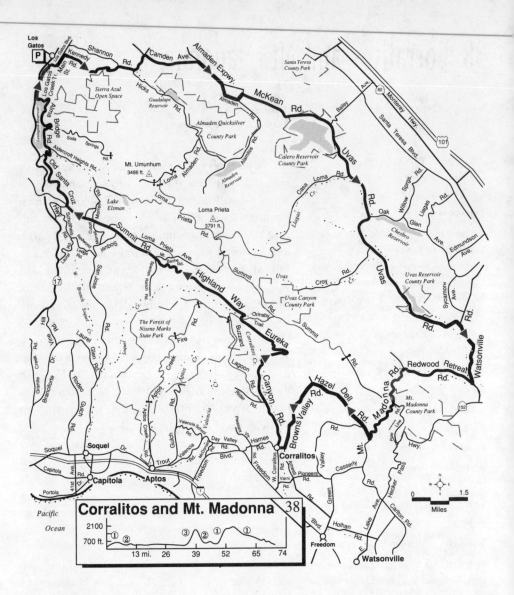

Corralitos and Mt. Madonna 38

2100
700 ft.

① ② ③ ② ① ①

13 mi. 26 39 52 65 74

40.9 Right on Hazel Dell Road at stop sign. Becomes Browns Valley Road.

44.5 Right to stay on Browns Valley Road at stop sign.

44.8 Right on Eureka Canyon Road at stop sign. Corralitos Store is last food stop until Summit Store. 53.7 Buzzard Lagoon Road junction and summit. Eureka Canyon Road becomes Highland Way.

There's a gradual climb in a canyon on quiet Hazel Dell Road, followed by a gentle descent on Browns Valley Road. Cross Corralitos Creek and ride into the town of Corralitos, where you'll find Corralitos Store on the corner. It specializes in sausages. Buy a sausage sandwich from the delicatessen to fuel the ride up Eureka Canyon Road. The road follows Corralitos Creek for several miles as it gradually winds its way up to a ridgetop, where it becomes Highland Way. Landslides occasionally

The earth shifted a foot or more on some sections of Summit Road east of Highway 17 during the 1989 Loma Prieta earthquake.

59.5 Left at stop sign. Highland Way becomes Summit Road. 61.5 Summit Store.

63.9 Right on Old Santa Cruz Highway. 66.3 Site of Holy City.

67.7 Right on Aldercroft Heights Road.

68.2 Left on Alma Bridge Road at T junction, crossing Los Gatos Creek bridge.

72.5 Right onto Los Gatos Creek Trail just before dam spillway, next to boat cabin.

74.2 Ride ends at East Main Street in Los Gatos.

make the bumpy road impassible for cars during rainy weather, so there may be some short dirt sections where slides have occurred.

Highland Way becomes Summit Road at the Mt. Bache Road junction. There's a brisk downhill to Soquel–San Jose Road and relief just beyond the intersection on your right at Summit Center Store. After a food stop and a soda, it's time to finish the ride with a fun descent on Old Santa Cruz Highway. The concrete road, covered by pavement, has a few bumpy sections, but it's generally lightly traveled. Don't miss the turn-off to Aldercroft Heights Road during the descent, or you'll wind up riding to Highway 17.

Ride the roller-coaster hills around Lexington Reservoir to the face of the dam, where there's a dirt trail that follows the spillway down. Walk your bike down the hill and continue on Los Gatos Creek Trail to the start of the ride. The trail has one other steep section that requires walking, but otherwise it's smooth enough to do on a road bike.

Afterward you might want to visit one of Los Gatos' popular coffeehouses on Main Street to celebrate a long ride through the wildlands of the Santa Cruz Mountains.

39 Hicks Road

Distance: 26 miles
Terrain: One steep hill
Traffic: Light to heavy

Mileage Log

0.0 Start mileage on East Main Street in downtown Los Gatos at the Highway 17 overpass next to Los Gatos Creek Trail. Ride east on East Main. Becomes Los Gatos Boulevard.

0.9 Right on Kennedy Road at traffic light. 1.5 South Kennedy on right, but keep left. 3.3 Summit.

4.2 Right on Shannon Road at stop sign.

4.9 Left on Hicks Road at stop sign.

5.9 Right on Camden Avenue at traffic light. 6.6 Summit.

8.3 Right on Almaden Expressway at traffic light.

10.0 Right on Almaden Road at traffic light. 12.4 Loma Almaden, Opry House, museum on left. 12.9 Road name changes to Alamitos Road at Alamitos Creek.

14.5 Right on Hicks Road. 15.0 Begin steep 1.2-mile climb. 16.2 Summit and Mt. Umunhum Road (also called Loma Almaden Road) on left. Begin steep, hazardous descent.

21.4 Left on Shannon Road. 22.6 Summit.

24.0 Keep left, continuing on Shannon Road at stop sign.

The sprawling city of San Jose extends south through Coyote Valley like the tentacle of an octopus, but it hasn't yet encroached upon the historic mining camp of New Almaden. Bicycle riding here can be a pleasant experience.

If not for New Almaden's mercury mines, we might not have had a California gold rush. Mercury is essential for smelting gold ore. Cinnabar, the red rock from which mercury is derived, was discovered by Antonio Suñol of San Jose in the hills above New Almaden. Suñol made his find after hearing stories about the distinctive red rock from the local Indians. A Mexican cavalry officer confirmed the location in 1845. Alexander Forbes opened the first mine in 1851.

Today the land surrounding the mines comprises the Almaden Quicksilver County Park. The park's mercury mines are mostly located along Los Capitancillos Ridge. Mexican, Chinese, and Cornish miners drilled into the hills to depths well below sea level.

All the mines have long since shut down, and today New Almaden is a quiet rural village. In 1974, Santa Clara County purchased 3,598 acres of the mining area for a park. On the left, just beyond the Opry House, there's a small museum you can visit (Saturdays, noon to 4:00 P.M.) to learn more about the mines. The park has miles of trails for hiking and horseback riding, but they're closed to bicycling.

As you ride up Hicks Road, now is a good time to imagine what life must have been like for the early-day miners. They might have considered the difficult 15-percent grade on Hicks a fun way to spend a Sunday afternoon, compared to the hard labor of mining.

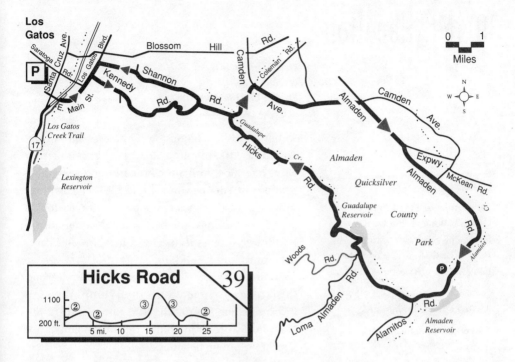

Hicks Road 39

24.8 Left on Los Gatos Boulevard at traffic light. Becomes East Main Street.

26.1 Ride ends at Los Gatos Creek Trail trailhead and Highway 17 overpass.

Hicks Road was built by Santa Clara County in 1868, at the behest of Thomas Hicks. He and his wife Josepha Burnell came into possession of 160 acres of land near what is now Hicks Road. They asked the county to build a road for local landowners. Hicks worked hard to have the road built, gaining support among local residents for his petition. The road was improved in 1878 and again in 1895.

Use caution riding down the northern slope of Hicks Road, which has even steeper sections than the southern slope. The ride up Shannon Road will seem easy after Hicks. For more local history, you can visit Forbes Flour Mill museum next to Highway 17 at Church and Main, the first business in Los Gatos in 1850, and the Los Gatos Museum at the corner of Main and Tate.

40 Mt. Hamilton

Distance: 104 miles
Terrain: Hilly
Traffic: Light to moderate

Mileage Log

0.0 Start mileage in Milpitas on Calaveras Boulevard at Calaveras Court, one block east of North Victoria Drive. Ride east on Calaveras Boulevard, which becomes Calaveras Road.

0.6 Right on Piedmont Road.

4.4 Left on Penitencia Creek Road at traffic light.

4.9 Right on Toyon Avenue.

5.8 Left on McKee Road at stop sign.

6.3 Left on Alum Rock Avenue at stop sign.

6.6 Right on Mount Hamilton Road. 8.4 Crothers Road junction on left. Descends to Alum Rock Park. 12.5 Begin 1.8-mile descent. 14.0 Quimby Road on right. Goes to San Jose. 14.2 Joseph D. Grant County Park on right. Restrooms, fountain, history museum. 17.5 Begin 0.9-mile descent to Smith Creek. 19.8 Kincaid Road on left. 20.7 Giant manzanita on left.

24.7 Summit. Water available from faucet outside house on right. Observatory uphill to right. Public display open most days. View point. 25.5 Begin descent. 27.6 Emergency water from spring on right. 29.9 End descent at Isabel Creek. Begin .6-mile

Although it's the highest and longest climb in the Bay Area, Mt. Hamilton Road is a long way from being the most difficult climb around. Being able to tell your friends you rode to the Mt. Hamilton summit at 4,209 feet isn't the only reason to do this ride. In the spring—the best time for riding here—wildflowers give a spectacular color show on a backdrop of rolling green hills.

On this ride you'll climb to the summit, descend the eastern slope, and then loop through Livermore and Sunol. The wild eastern side of Mt. Hamilton offers uncompromising beauty, but almost no public facilities.

The road was built in 1876 to accommodate horses hauling heavy equipment, which is why the climb has a steady 5–7 percent grade, with the exception of two descents. On weekends there's a fair amount of traffic in the early going, but it thins out after several miles. The first of two short descents on the climb brings you to Joseph D. Grant County Park, where there's a restroom, drinking fountains, and an old ranch house that doubles as a museum and park headquarters. The road climbs past the park entrance to offer a spectacular overlook of Halls Valley. In the spring, white wildflowers carpet the valley floor, looking like freshly fallen snow. Watch for hawks, kites, turkey vultures, bluebirds, kingbirds, woodpeckers, horned larks, and golden eagles soaring over the valley. Roadrunners have been seen on warm days.

Following the second descent, to Smith Creek, you'll pass giant manzanita, a bush identified by its polished dark-cinnamon-colored limbs. The last 6 miles has many hairpin turns and the best views of Santa Clara Valley.

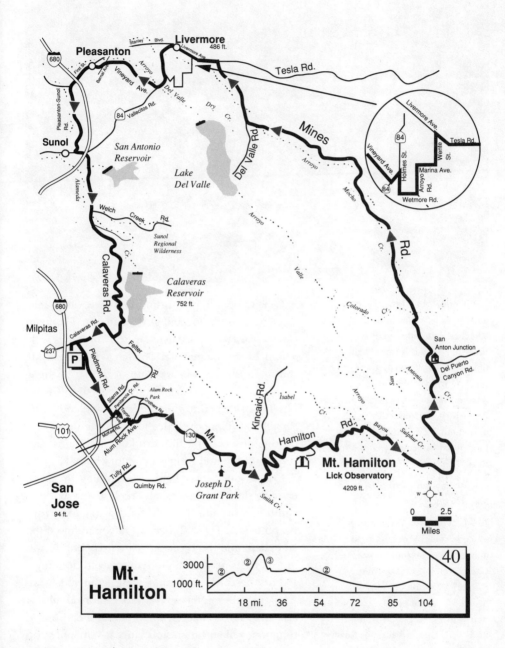

680
Stanley Blvd.
Pleasanton
First St.
Bernal Ave.
Vineyard Ave.
Arroyo
Del Valle
Livermore 486 ft.
Livermore Ave.
Tesla Rd.

84 Vallecitos Rd.
Dry Cr.
Mines
Arroyo

Livermore Ave.
84
Vineyard Ave.
Holmes St.
Wente St.
Tesla Rd.
Marina Ave.
Arroyo Rd.
84
Wetmore Rd.

Pleasanton-Sunol Rd.
Sunol
San Antonio Reservoir
Lake Del Valle
Del Valle Rd.

Alameda
Welch Creek Rd.
Sunol Regional Wilderness

Mocho
Cr.
Rd.

Calaveras Rd.
Calaveras Reservoir 752 ft.
Valle
Colorado Cr.
San Antonio
San
Cr.

680
Milpitas
Calaveras Rd.
Felter Rd.

San Anton Junction
Del Puerto Canyon Cr.
Canyon Rd.

237
P
Piedmont Rd.
Sierra Rd.
Penitencia Cr. Rd.
Alum Rock Park
Crothers Rd.
Toyon
McKee Rd.

Kincaid Rd.
Isabel Cr.
Arroyo
Hamilton Rd.
Bayou
Sulphur Cr.

101
Alum Rock Ave.
130 Mt.
Tully Rd.
Quimby Rd.
Hamilton Rd.

Mt. Hamilton
Lick Observatory
4209 ft.

San Jose 94 ft.
Joseph D. Grant Park
Smith Cr.

N W E S
0   2.5
Miles

Mt. Hamilton
3000
1000 ft.
② ② ③ ②
18 mi.   36   54   72   85   104

40

climb followed by 1-mile descent. 33.1 Begin 0.3-mile climb. 36.2 Begin 0.8-mile climb followed by 0.7-mile descent. 38.0 San Antonio Valley flower display. 42.8 San Anton Junction bar. Del Puerto Canyon Road on right goes to Patterson. 43.9 Begin 1.9-mile climb. 46.9 Begin 1.1-mile climb. 50.9 Alameda County Line. Road name changes to Mines Road. 62.5 Begin 3.5-mile descent.

66.9 Right at stop sign, staying on Mines Road.

70.3 Left on Tesla Road at stop sign, which becomes Vineyard Road in 0.1 miles. (Alternate route bypassing Livermore: 71.4 Left on Wente Street. 72.3 Wente becomes Marina Avenue. 73.2 Left on Arroyo Road at stop sign. 74.0 Right on Wetmore Road. 75.0 Left on Vallecitos Road, Highway 84, at stop sign. 75.4 Right on Vineyard Avenue.)

72.1 Left on College Avenue across the street from City Hall and police station.

73.3 Left on South 4th Street.

Lick Observatory housing and five white telescope domes are located at the summit. The main observatory was constructed in 1887 by James Lick, a real estate magnate. A 36-inch refractor inside the main observatory was one of the largest telescopes of its day. Turn right to reach the main observatory, open to the public on weekends, 1:00 to 5:00 P.M. The post office lobby at the north end of the observatory has drinking fountains and restrooms, open during observatory hours.

Check your brakes before descending the steep eastern slope. Cross Isabel Creek at the bottom, climb a short hill, and descend again to Arroyo Bayou Creek. The old road below you followed the creekbed and had numerous fords, but it was moved to its present alignment to avoid flooding.

The best wildflower viewing comes at San Antonio Valley, after several more short climbs. A few miles farther along, you'll come to San Anton Junction, a likely lunch stop, since it's the only stop until Livermore. The bar sells everything from hamburgers to soup, soda, beer, and candy bars.

Opposite: Switchbacks on Mt. Hamilton Road make the climb relatively easy.

Left: "Car Man" at San Anton Junction was made from old parts.

73.4 Left at traffic light on Holmes Street, Highway 84. 74.3 Shopping center with gas station, liquor store, and grocery store.

75.5 Keep right on Highway 84 at junction.

75.8 Right on Vineyard Avenue.

80.0 Left on Bernal Avenue at stop sign.

80.1 Right on Vineyard Avenue at stop sign.

80.9 Left on First Street at traffic light. 81.8 Oak Hills Shopping Center.

82.9 Left on Pleasanton-Sunol Road after passing under Interstate 680.

86.5 Left on Highway 84 at stop sign. 87.2 Pass under Interstate 680. Becomes Calaveras Road. 87.5 Cork oak trees on right. 91.2 Start climb. False summit at 94.1 miles. 100.8 End climb.

101.2 Right on Calaveras Road at stop sign. 102.0 Ed R. Levin County Park. Water fountains, restrooms.

104.2 End ride at Calaveras Court.

Continue to Livermore on Mines Road, which follows Arroyo Mocho Creek in a narrow canyon. There's a 2-mile and a 1-mile climb before coming to a long, fast descent to Livermore Valley's vineyards.

An alternate route (taking 0.5 miles off the total distance) that avoids Livermore is included here, or you can visit the town and stock up on food. The ride continues through vineyards into Pleasanton.

Finally, there's the final long climb up traffic-free Calaveras Road to a ridge at 1,000 feet. This is a good time to enjoy the blue waters of Calaveras Reservoir and contemplate the five-course meal you'll have after the ride.

41 Santa Cruz

Distance: 51 miles
Terrain: Hilly
Traffic: Light to moderate

Mileage Log

0.0 Start mileage on Los Gatos Creek Trail, located at the junction of East Main Street and the Highway 17 overpass in downtown Los Gatos. Walk bike through barrier and ride downhill on dirt trail. Parking available at Lexington Dam if you don't want to ride on the trail. 1.3 Short, steep climb. 1.5 Climb face of Lexington Dam on trail. Stay left of spillway.

1.6 Left on Alma Bridge Road after going through barrier. 4.5 Soda Springs Road.

5.9 Keep right at Aldercroft Heights Road junction. Becomes Aldercroft Heights Road.

6.5 Left on Old Santa Cruz Highway at yield sign. 7.8 Holy City site. 9.0 Mountain Charlie Road on right.

10.1 Left on Summit Road at stop sign.

11.5 Right on Morrell Cutoff. 12.4 creek.

13.3 Right on Soquel–San Jose Road at stop sign.

19.8 Right on Laurel Glen Road at Casalegno Store. 22.1 Summit. Becomes Mountain View Road.

23.0 Left on Branciforte Drive at stop sign. 25.9 Granite Creek Road.

You can ride to Santa Cruz from the South Bay along many different routes, but this route is one of the most scenic, least traveled, and easiest to negotiate. Unless you have legs of steel, you will probably have to walk up the steep slope of Lexington Dam, and there's a 1.6-mile stretch of dirt road with a short, steep climb. Be sure to bring your sense of adventure for these sections.

The ride starts in downtown Los Gatos where Los Gatos Creek Trail joins East Main Street at the Highway 17 overpass. The wide, mostly flat, trail follows Los Gatos Creek through Los Gatos Canyon. You'll see many hikers and cyclists on the well-known trail. If you go right at the bottom of the first short hill that starts the ride, you can see Forbes Flour Mill museum in about 200 yards, the first business in Los Gatos in 1850.

The trail follows the route of South Pacific Coast Railroad, which went through the canyon from late 1880 until 1940, when it was disbanded. The railroad continued into Aldercroft Canyon and then through eight tunnels bored into the Santa Cruz Mountains. If only the tunnels were still open for bicycling! Today you can take a train ride from Felton's Roaring Camp to Santa Cruz, following the original route. Call (408) 335-4484 for information.

Go left across the dam and begin a roller-coaster ride on Alma Bridge Road, which winds around the reservoir. A long climb begins when you cross Los Gatos Creek. Alma Bridge Road merges here with Aldercroft Heights Road. Author Jack London spent summers at a cabin on what is now Santa Cruz Water Company land, near the second tunnel entrance at Morrell Road and Los Gatos Creek.

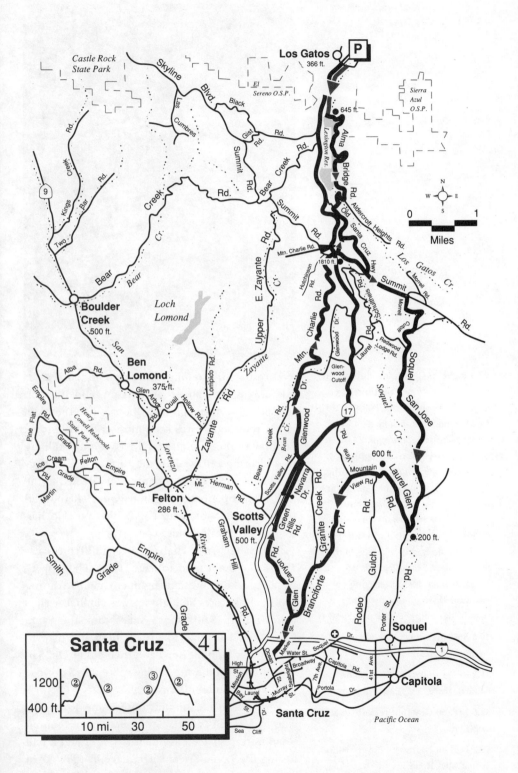

Castle Rock
State Park

Skyline Blvd.

Los Gatos
366 ft.

P

El Sereno O.S.P.

Sierra Azul O.S.P.

645 ft.

Black

Las Cumbres

Gist Rd.

Bear Creek Rd.

Lexington Res.

Alma Bridge Rd.

Aldercroft Heights Rd.

Los Gatos Cr.

N
W   E
S

0   1
Miles

Rd.

Creek

Kings

Two Bar

Creek Cr.

Summit Rd.

Creek Rd.

Summit Rd.

Mtn. Charlie Rd.

1810 ft.

Old Santa Cruz Hwy.

Summit

Morrell Rd.

9

Bear

Bear

Bear Cr.

Loch
Lomond

Upper E. Zayante

Hutchinson Rd.

Mtn. Charlie Rd.

Schultheis Rd.

Laurel Rd.

Morrell Rd.

Soquel

Rd.

Boulder
Creek
500 ft.

San

Ben
Lomond
375 ft.

Glen Arbor Rd.

Quail Hollow Rd.

Lompico Rd.

Zayante Rd.

Glenwood Dr.

Glenwood Cutoff

Redwood Lodge Rd.

Soquel San Jose

Alba   Rd.

Empire

Pine Flat Rd.

Grade

Henry
Cowell Redwoods
State Park

Lorenzo

Glenwood Dr.

17

Soquel Cr.

600 ft.

Laurel Glen Rd.

Ice Cream Grade

Felton Grade

Empire   Rd.

Zayante

Bean Creek Rd.

Scotts Valley Rd.

Navarra Dr.

Granite Creek Rd.

Mountain
View Rd.

Rd.

Martin

Mt. Herman Rd.

Green Hills Rd.

200 ft.

Felton
286 ft.

Scotts
Valley
500 ft.

Rodeo Gulch Rd.

Smith   Grade

Empire   Grade

River

Graham Hill Rd.

Canyon Rd.

Glen St.

Branciforte

Soquel

Porter St.

Soquel

Capitola

1

Pacific Ocean

Santa Cruz

High St.

Mission St.

Bay St.

Laurel
Dr.

Ocean
St.

Market St.

Murray St.

Water St.

Seabright

Broadway

Soquel

7th Ave.

Capitola Rd.

Portola Dr.

41st Ave.

Sea Cliff

Los Gatos Creek Trail climbs the face of Lexington Dam.

27.6 Right on Glen Canyon Road. (If going to Santa Cruz, continue straight on Branciforte. 28.3 Left on Goss Avenue at stop sign. 28.4 Right on Branciforte at stop sign. 29.0 Left on Water Street at traffic light. 29.2 Right on Seabright Avenue at traffic light. 29.3 Left on Soquel Avenue at traffic light, then right back onto Seabright. 30.2 Sullivan's Bike Shop on right just beyond Murray Street. To get to the Boardwalk, take Murray Street toward Santa Cruz for 0.3 miles. Pick up sidewalk starting on East Cliff Drive on left, down to railroad bridge and pedestrian walkway.)

30.6 Straight at stop sign. Becomes Green Hills Road.

31.9 Ride through barrier. Becomes Navarra Drive.

32.6 Left on Granite Creek Road at stop sign.

32.7 Left on Highway 17 overpass to Scotts Valley Road.

Fortunately, the long climb on Old Santa Cruz Highway is only about 4-6 percent, and traffic is usually light. Although many houses line the road, dense redwood groves keep most of them hidden. Halfway to the summit you'll pass a long building in a clearing on the left, the former site of Holy City. The quirky little community flourished in the 1930s. The opening of Highway 17 in 1940 reduced traffic on Old Santa Cruz Highway to a trickle, hastening the town's demise.

Old Santa Cruz Highway was, until the early 1940s, the main road to Santa Cruz. Highway 17 began to take its present alignment and size during the 1930s. Before the highways were built, travelers coming from Santa Clara Valley took the Santa Cruz Gap Turnpike toll road, built in 1858, to present-day Summit Road and then either Old San Jose Road (following today's Soquel–San Jose Road) or Mountain Charlie toll road.

Turn left at the summit on Summit Road and ride to Morrell Cutoff. Some sections of Summit Road were displaced as much as a foot and a half during the Loma Prieta earthquake in 1989. Turn

Road Rides

32.9 Right on Scotts Valley Road at traffic light. Then immediate shallow left at traffic light onto Glenwood Highway. 34.8 Bean Creek Road.

35.7 Left on Mountain Charlie Road. The climb has three steep pitches of about 15 percent, 200 yards each. 39.9 Road levels. 40.4 Spring on left.

40.9 Straight onto Summit Road at stop sign. 41.1 Cross Highway 17 on Summit Road overpass. Left at stop sign and then immediate left onto Mountain Charlie Road.

41.9 Left on Old Santa Cruz Highway at stop sign.

44.5 Right on Aldercroft Heights Road.

45.1 Left onto Alma Bridge Road after crossing Los Gatos Creek.

49.3 Walk down Los Gatos Trail on Lexington Dam.

51.0 End ride at East Main Street.

right on Morrell, and begin a steep, bumpy descent to Laurel Creek. The secluded road climbs gradually back to Soquel–San Jose Road. (If you want to stop at Summit Store, continue straight on Summit Road a short distance.) Begin a long, gradual descent on tree-lined Soquel–San Jose Road to Laurel Glen Road. Look for Casalegno Store at the intersection.

There's a moderate climb on Laurel Glen Road, followed by a gradual descent to Branciforte Drive. At Branciforte and Glen Canyon Road you can either ride into Santa Cruz on Branciforte according to route directions, or ride home by Glen Canyon Road. Glen Canyon climbs gradually to Highway 17, where you'll take Green Hills Road, which becomes Navarra Drive, and then bridge over Highway 17 to Scotts Valley Road.

Turn right and then left at the traffic lights on Scotts Valley Road to begin a gradual climb on Glenwood Highway. Spacious fields give way to redwoods as you climb the bumpy concrete road, which was built around 1914. Turn left on Mountain Charlie Road, where you'll have a chance to test your legs on occasional short, steep stretches. Charles Henry "Mountain Charlie" McKiernan built the road in 1858 and charged a toll. It must have been a daring adventure to take a wagon down the road because some sections are as steep as 17 percent. But the road climbs like a staircase, with level sections you can rest on. Don't miss the blue silo on your left; a creative designer turned it into a house. At the top of the climb, you'll see Mountain Charlie's homesite on the right. Near here in 1854 the early settler got into a fight with a grizzly bear, narrowly escaping with his life. The road levels here and takes you to Summit Road, crossing Highway 17 by overpass. Take Mountain Charlie Road down to Old Santa Cruz Highway and retrace your route to downtown Los Gatos.

42 Stevens Creek Reservoir

Distance: 11 miles
Terrain: One moderate hill
Traffic: Moderate

Riding around Stevens Creek Reservoir after work has become a popular pastime for cyclists in Silicon Valley. Scenic hillsides, invigorating climbs, and a park setting offer a welcome change from the crowded valley. Start the ride at Lower Stevens Creek County Park on Stevens Canyon Road. If you're interested in mountain bike riding, you can ride up the power-line road, where you'll have spectacular views from the ridgetop, and over to Fremont Older Open Space Preserve. The power-line trail starts across the road from park headquarters. It follows Stevens Creek for 0.3 miles before rising steeply.

For the road ride, turn left onto Stevens Canyon Road from the parking lot at park headquarters. Stevens Canyon Road rolls along for several miles, with mostly easy climbs. The road follows Stevens Creek through a narrow canyon where extensive flooding occurred during the winter of 1982–83. Begin a moderate climb at Mt. Eden Road, which snakes up to a ridge overlooking a former orchard, now populated by pink mansions. The historic Garrod Horse Ranch on the left at the summit permits bicycles to ride through to reach trails in Fremont Older. Remember, bikes must yield to equestrians.

A steep descent is followed by a flat section and a brisk downhill on Pierce Road to Comer Drive. Just before turning left onto Comer you'll pass Kennedy Vineyards, one of the last valley vineyards in an urban setting. Turn right onto Arroyo de Arguello and return to where you started on residential streets.

Mileage Log

0.0 Start at parking lot next to park headquarters for Lower Stevens Creek County Park. Restrooms, water fountain. Left at stop sign onto Stevens Canyon Road. 0.6 Stevens Creek Dam parking lot. 1.0 Montebello Road on right. Climbs to Black Mountain and connects with Page Mill.

2.4 Keep left onto Mt. Eden Road at stop sign. Stevens Canyon Road goes right. (Pavement on Stevens Canyon Road ends in 3.7 miles. It's a gentle climb through beautiful tree-lined canyon.) Begin 0.8-mile climb. 3.2 Top of hill. 3.9 Check brakes. Steep downhill.

4.7 Left on Pierce Road at stop sign.

6.1 Left on Comer Drive. Watch for row of pine trees.

6.2 Right on Arroyo de Arguello.

7.2 Left on Via Roncole at stop sign.

7.3 Left on Prospect Road at stop sign.

7.6 Keep right on Stelling Road. Prospect Road goes to Fremont Older Open Space Preserve and popular mountain bike trail to Lower Stevens Creek Park.

8.1 Left on Rainbow Drive at traffic light.

8.6 Right on Bubb Road at stop sign.

Road Rides

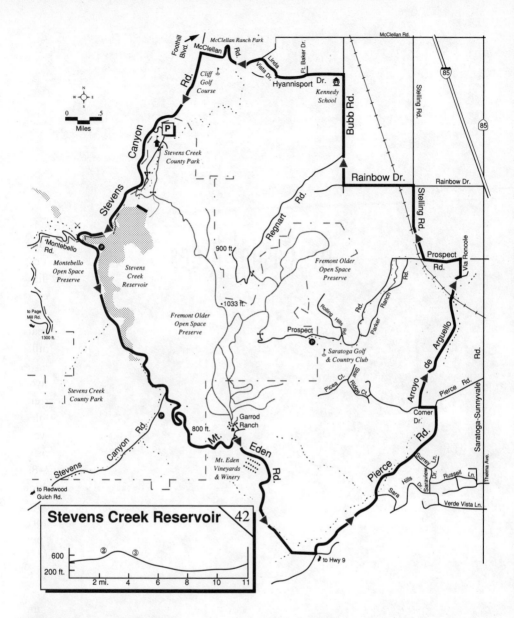

Stevens Creek Reservoir 42

9.3 Left on Hyannisport at stop sign.

9.6 Keep left on Hyannisport.

9.8 Right on Linda Vista Drive.

10.0 Left on McClellan Road at stop sign.

10.6 Left on Stevens Canyon Road at stop sign.

11.3 Left into Lower Stevens Creek County Park parking lot. Ride ends.

III. Casual Rides

43 Coyote Hills Regional Park

Distance: Up to 21 miles
Terrain: Flat
Traffic: Bicyclists, hikers

Mileage Log

LOOP:

0.0 State mileage at the visitor center in Coyote Hills Regional Park. Ride southeast toward Patterson Ranch Road.

0.3 Right at parking lot and path, where you'll see restrooms and a picnic area. Stay on paved path at all times for this loop.

1.0 Right at junction. Apay Way on left. It's 1.6 miles from here to Highway 84 and the National Wildlife Center.

2.6 Keep right to return to visitor center.

3.4 End loop at visitor center.

FROM VISITOR CENTER TO NILES CANYON ON ALAMEDA CREEK REGIONAL TRAIL:

0.0 Start at visitor center and ride toward Bay on Bayview Trail.

0.8 Right at junction to reach Alameda Creek Regional Trail, followed by immediate right onto Alameda Creek path. 2.5 Union City Boulevard. 3.2 Train tracks. 3.9 Alvarado Boulevard. 4.1 Interstate 880. 5.8 Decoto Road 6.6 Isherwood Way. 9.3 BART and train tracks. 10.3 Mission Boulevard. 10.5 Old Canyon Road Bridge. End of trail at Niles Canyon. Return by same route.

21.0 End of ride.

Coyote Hills Regional Park offers one of the most diverse geographical settings in the Bay Area. A knoll in the park overlooking the Bay is complemented by nearby marshes, a history museum, miles of bike paths, picnic benches, and abundant wildlife.

You'll understand why the Ohlone people settled here after you tour the peaceful marshes and bayshore. Shell mounds left by the Indians demonstrate the fruitful bounty they found in nearby Alameda Creek and the Bay. Reeds from the marsh were used to make boats, baskets, and huts, and the hills have rock suitable for making arrowheads. You can see Ohlone culture and artifacts on display at park headquarters and then tour the marshes.

A gently rolling path winds around the base of the hills in the 1,021-acre park next to Dumbarton Bridge. For a longer ride, take the path along Alameda Creek; Alameda Creek Regional Trail passes under all road and train bridges. The Army Corps of Engineers built the path as part of a flood control project in 1973. Stay on the south side of the creek both directions. The north side is designated for horseback riding. You'll see the white-plumed egret, great blue heron, and a variety of ducks feeding along the creek.

For an interesting side trip, visit Ardenwood Historic Farm. To get there from the trail, take Ardenwood Boulevard, the first bridge. It's about a mile to the park entrance. The farm depicts life in the 1880s. Land is tilled by horse and plow, cows are milked by hand, and the farmhouse has furniture from the period. You can tour on foot or go by horse-drawn flat car on railroad tracks. The park is open April through November, and admission is $5 on weekends, less on weekdays. For more information, call (510) 796-0663.

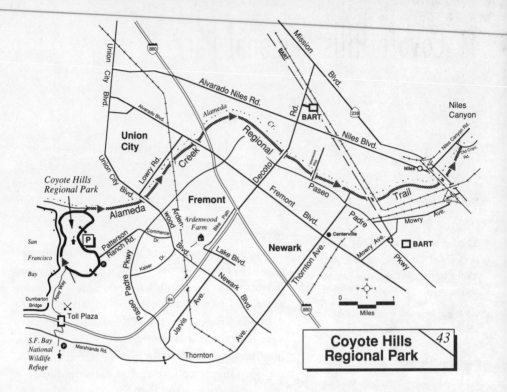

Coyote Hills Regional Park 43

Six miles from Coyote Hills, ride under Interstate 880 and then turn south. The path passes rock quarries and railroad yards. In the nearby Niles District during World War I, Charlie Chaplin made five of his early movies with Gloria Swanson.

Apay Way, a dirt road in the park, connects with the National Wildlife Refuge south of Dumbarton Bridge. Dense brush and dill growing along the road provide an ideal habitat for deer and bobcats. Cross Highway 84 on a pedestrian bridge over the toll booths.

Cyclists coming from Palo Alto can take a recreation path over Dumbarton Bridge and continue east on a frontage road. The 1.6-mile span and the Golden Gate Bridge provide the only bike routes over San Francisco Bay.

Guided tours of the refuge are offered by bike and on foot. For more information, call (510) 795-9385. Coyote Hills Regional Park and Alameda Creek Regional Trail are administered by the East Bay Regional Park District, 2950 Peralta Court, Oakland, CA 94605; phone (510) 635-0135.

Casual Rides

44 Lafayette-Moraga Regional Trail

Distance: 14 miles
Terrain: Mostly flat
Traffic: Light to moderate; hikers

The Bay Area Rapid Transit system (BART) opens new dimensions in bike riding. The light rail line is a fun, easy way to get around without driving. Here's just one example: Take BART to the town of Orinda and make a loop back to the Lafayette BART station. The 14-mile ride follows Lafayette-Moraga Regional Trail, the former right-of-way of the Sacramento Northern Railroad. The paved path winds through a valley and a secluded canyon as it follows Las Trampas Creek.

Bikes are permitted on BART all day on weekends and holidays, but you must have a bike permit. You can get a temporary permit at any primary station. Restrictions apply during the commute rush hour.

Leave the Orinda BART station by the Moraga Way ramp and ride to Moraga, merging with traffic on Moraga Way under the Highway 24 overpass. The two-lane road has a broad shoulder all the way to the trail. There's a gradual 2.2-mile climb followed by a descent to the town of Moraga.

At the traffic light, turn left onto Moraga Road. In less than a half-mile there's another traffic light at St. Mary's Road, where you'll turn right and enter Moraga Commons Park to pick up the Lafayette-Moraga Trail. The park has a playground, restrooms, and drinking fountains.

Cross a wooden bridge and stay on the path for the next 5.8 miles. Although you're starting the path inside the park, the trail originates about a mile to the south.

The East Bay Regional Park trail opened in 1976. The route was first used by mule trains hauling redwood from Oakland to Sacramento and later was a right-of-way for the Sacramento Northern Railway before becoming a trail. Sacramento Northern

Mileage Log

0.0 Start ride at the Orinda BART station, and take Moraga Way to the town of Moraga.

4.7 Left on Moraga Road at traffic light.

5.1 Right at traffic light at St. Mary's Road; immediately enter Moraga Commons Park and pick up the Lafayette-Moraga Trail. 9.9 Water fountain.

11.0 Left on Olympic Boulevard, exiting park. Immediately turn left onto Pleasant Hill Road at stop sign.

11.9 Left on Mt. Diablo Boulevard at traffic light.

13.6 Right on Happy Valley Road at traffic light (or right on Oak Hill Road at traffic light, then left on Deer Hill Road).

13.9 Right on Deer Hill Road to BART station. End ride.

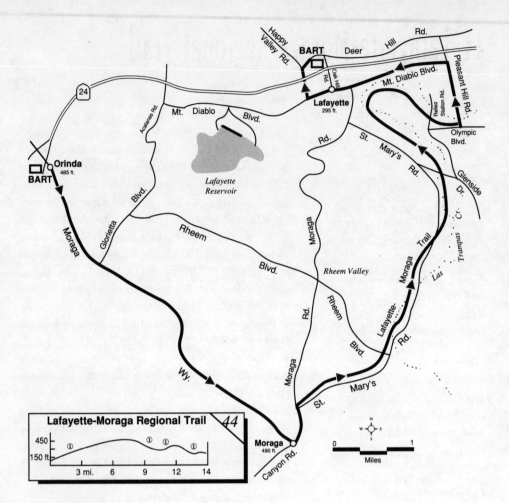

Happy Valley Rd.

BART

Deer Hill Rd.

Pleasant Hill Rd.

24

Oak Hill Rd.

Lafayette
295 ft.

Mt. Diablo Blvd.

Relez Station Rd.

Acalanes Rd.

Mt. Diablo Blvd.

Olympic Blvd.

Orinda
485 ft.

BART

St. Mary's Rd.

Glorietta Blvd.

Rheem Blvd.

Moraga

Moraga Rd.

Lafayette Reservoir

Rheem Valley

Moraga Trail

Glenside Dr.

Las Trampas Cr.

Lafayette-Moraga Rd.

Rheem Blvd.

Moraga Rd.

Wy.

Mary's

St.

Moraga
490 ft.

Canyon Rd.

Lafayette-Moraga Regional Trail *44*

450

150 ft

3 mi.   6   9   12   14

N
W   E
S

0   1

Miles

carried freight and passengers between San Francisco and Sacramento on electric trains from 1913 until 1941.

The trail crosses driveways and some roads, where there are stop signs. Use caution crossing busy St. Mary's Road. The trail ends at a parking lot across from Reliez Station Road. On the far side of the parking lot, turn left on Olympic Boulevard and left again, riding north on Pleasant Hill Road.

Turn left on Mt. Diablo Boulevard and ride through downtown Lafayette. Turn right on Oak Hill Road at the traffic light, or right at Happy Valley Road, to reach BART.

Rails to Trails Conservancy, a national nonprofit organization based in Washington D.C., assists communities and organizations dedicated to preserving railroad rights-of-way for recreational use. More than 160 trails have been built on abandoned railroad corridors nationwide, totaling 2,400 miles.

The largest rail-to-trail project in the Bay Area is the San Ramon Valley Ironhorse Trail. Southern Pacific owned the rail line from the time it was established in the 1890s until it was abandoned about 10 years ago. When finished, the trail will extend 16 miles through San Ramon, Danville, Alamo, and Walnut Creek, and eventually join Ygnacio Canal in Walnut Creek.

45 San Leandro Creek Trail

Distance: 5 miles
Terrain: Flat
Traffic: Bicyclists, hikers

Mileage Log

0.0 Start mileage at Martin Luther King, Jr. Regional Shoreline visitor center, located 0.8 miles north of Swan Way on a dirt road. Ride south on San Leandro Creek Trail.

0.9 Left over San Leandro Creek on Hegenberger Road bridge, and then left again back on path.

1.9 Left on bridge over Elmhurst Creek. 2.6 Garretson Point. Restrooms and water. Turn around and retrace path. At visitor center continue on path headed west. Turn around at parking area next to Swan Way and return to visitor center.

5.2 End of ride.

Surprisingly, San Leandro Bay, located in an industrial area between the busy Nimitz Freeway and Oakland Airport, offers quiet solitude on a 1,218-acre nature preserve maintained by the East Bay Regional Park District.

At Martin Luther King, Jr. Regional Shoreline, which encompasses San Leandro Bay, you can hike, bicycle, bird watch, fish, sunbathe, and go boating. A fishing pier is located on Doolittle Drive, next to a boat launch, with Doolittle Beach farther north. Bike lanes extend the length of Doolittle Drive.

A bike trail in the park follows both sides of San Leandro Creek, passing warehouses and an open field. Watch for hikers strolling along the path, and keep your speed below 15 mph. Besides hikers, you might run over one of many ground squirrels that dart across the path.

In 1882, San Leandro Bay was a large marsh extending inland past what is now San Leandro Boulevard and west over most of today's Oakland Airport. In that year in this location a tragic train accident occurred. Tracks that ran just to the west of Doolittle Drive were constantly sinking into the mud. On the evening of September 11, a northbound South Pacific Coast freight train hit a submerged section of track and pitched over on its side into the bay mud. Fireman Dan Driscoll was pinned under the locomotive. In a scene reminiscent of Ken Kesey's novel *Sometimes a Great Notion*, the train crew worked desperately to free him before the tide rose, but to no avail.

The bridge was damaged in the 1906 earthquake and dismantled shortly afterward. Now there's a vehicle bridge where the train bridge stood. Trains carrying passengers between Oakland and Santa Cruz have long since quit running, and the marshy

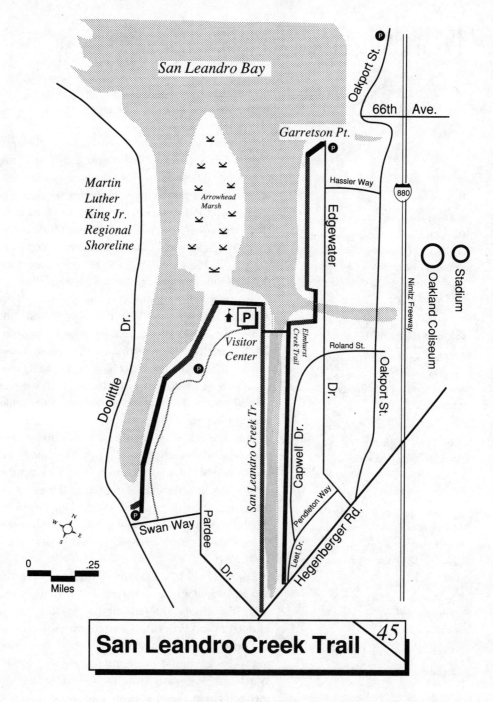

San Leandro Bay

Martin
Luther
King Jr.
Regional
Shoreline

Arrowhead
Marsh

Garretson Pt.

Oakport St.

66th Ave.

Hassler Way

880

Edgewater

Nimitz Freeway

Stadium
Oakland Coliseum

Doolittle Dr.

Visitor
Center

Elmhurst Creek Trail

Roland St.

Oakport St.

Dr.

San Leandro Creek Tr.

Capwell Dr.

Pendleton Way

Leet Dr.

Hegenberger Rd.

Swan Way

Pardee Dr.

N
W   E
S

0   .25
Miles

San Leandro Creek Trail 45

waters where the trainman died are airport run-
ways.

The shoreline park is easily accessible by public
transportation. Take BART to the Coliseum Station
and then Hegenberger Road south.

46 Walnut Creek Canals

Distance: 8 miles
Terrain: One short hill
Traffic: Bicyclists, hikers

Mileage Log

0.0 Start mileage at Marchbanks Drive on a path across the parking lot from golf course, in Walnut Creek's Heather Farms City Park. Ride northeast on Ygnacio Canal. 0.2 Lake on right.

0.3 Left. Cross road and take path to Contra Costa Canal.

0.4 Right on path after crossing Contra Costa Canal. 0.8 Bancroft Avenue. 2.0 Oak Grove Road. 2.7 Citrus Avenue.

2.8 Right at junction, picking up Shell Ridge Trail, which follows Ygnacio Canal. Begin climbing. 3.5 Tunnel under Ygnacio Valley Road. 4.4 Arbolado Drive.

4.6 Keep right along Ygnacio Canal. 4.7 Oak Grove Road. 5.5 Walnut Avenue. 6.9 San Miguel Park on right. 7.0 John Muir Memorial Hospital.

7.2 Cross Ygnacio Valley Road at signal light, turn right, and take sidewalk.

7.4 Left on Marchbanks Drive.

7.7 End ride at Heather Farms Park.

More than 15 miles of canals course through Walnut Creek, Pleasant Hill, and Concord, offering casual, mostly flat bike rides away from busy streets. It isn't Venice, but the irrigation canals are popular, drawing walkers, runners, skateboarders, bicyclists, and roller skaters. The eight-foot-wide recreation paths mostly follow canals. Although the paths are bisected by busy streets, they pass through quiet residential neighborhoods.

An extensive irrigation project was started in Walnut Creek in the 1930s to supply San Ramon Valley, but World War II delayed completion until 1952. Water is imported from the Sacramento and San Joaquin Delta near Rock Slough, where it eventually reaches Martinez to be treated and used as drinking water. Fishing and swimming in the canal are prohibited.

The tour starts in Heather Farms Park, where there's a swimming pool, playground, concession stand, baseball diamond, and a lake. Pick up the path where it intersects Marchbanks Drive, across the street from the golf course parking lot. Ride north, turn left in a parking lot, and you'll see Contra Costa Canal across a wooden bridge. Turn right here.

The only hill is a 300-yard climb. It comes after Citrus Avenue and a right turn at a T-intersection. After the climb, ride through a narrow tunnel under Ygnacio Valley Road, where the path continues next to a golf course and Ygnacio Canal, passing through quiet residential neighborhoods. Watch out for blind corners, and ride carefully through the barriers at every intersection; they're barely wide enough for standard handlebars.

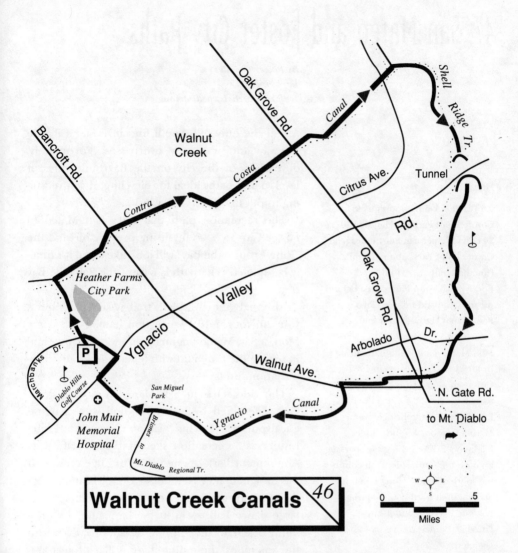

Walnut Creek Canals 46

Finish the loop by passing John Muir Memorial Hospital and crossing busy Ygnacio Valley Road at a signal crosswalk. Ride on the sidewalk to Marchbanks Drive to complete the loop.

Contra Costa Canal is managed by East Bay Regional Park District, and Ygnacio Canal by the Walnut Creek parks department.

47 San Mateo and Foster City Paths

Distance: 14 miles
Terrain: Flat
Traffic: Bicyclists, pedestrians

Mileage Log

0.0 Watch for direction signs to Coyote Point Park off Highway 101. $4 entry fee per car. Start mileage at Coyote Point Park, about 0.6 miles from park entrance, in the Eucalyptus Group Picnic area behind the museum and next to Coyote Point Yacht Harbor. Ride southeast through the parking lot. 0.1 Gerry Mon Memorial Bike Path, dedicated by the city of San Mateo in 1987. 1.2 Cross San Mateo Creek. Watch for narrow barriers. 2.1 Cross the old East Third Avenue Bridge over Marina Lagoon. 4.0 Ride under Highway 92. The fishing pier parking lot is on the south side. Path continues south and west along Belmont Slough, then north along Marina Lagoon. 9.9 Ride under East Hillsdale Boulevard overpass and keep left.

10.9 Ride under Highway 92 overpass and then take first right on sidewalk into parking lot. Exit parking lot onto Fashion Island Boulevard on left. Take right turn from parking lot.

11.1 Left on Mariner's Island Boulevard at traffic light.

12.1 Left on East Third Avenue at traffic light. Right onto recreation path, continuing north back to start.

14.3 Ride ends at Coyote Point Park.

About the only hills you'll find in Foster City are freeway and waterway overpasses. Fortunately, developers of the city on the Bay built miles of level, paved paths ideal for bicycling, if you're willing to put up with a little wind.

The recreation path that links San Mateo to Foster City gives a tantalizing preview of what the "Ring Around the Bay" will look like when it's finally completed. The path is part of the 250-mile Bay trail.

Although the complete trail is still years away, you can tour a 10-mile section named for Gerry Mon, a San Mateo engineer who was instrumental in having the trail built with federal and state transportation funds.

The ride starts in San Mateo at Coyote Point Park, identified by its rocky knoll with a dense eucalyptus grove. This location has an interesting history as a recreation site. In 1922, Pacific City Amusement Park opened here to huge crowds. It was designed after New York's Coney Island: attendants could ride a roller coaster, do the tango in a large dance hall, swim in the bay, sunbathe on a sandy beach, or dine in fine restaurants. Even with the amenities, the multimillion dollar project lasted only two years; the initial excitement wore off, and attendance dropped. A fire destroyed one-quarter of the grounds, and sewage in the bay closed the beach.

Today's park has a clean, sandy beach, the bay water isn't so polluted, and you can still find a fancy restaurant (The Castaways) with a view of jets landing at San Francisco airport. There's also an excellent nature museum, a golf course, and a marina.

The bike path starts from the marina on the Bay and extends south to Foster City and Belmont

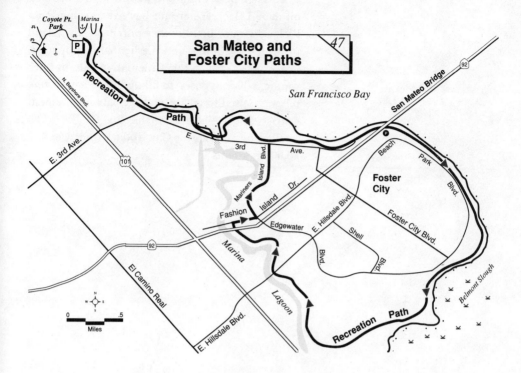

Slough. You can ride at least 9 miles one way along the Bay, almost all the way around Foster City. A major obstacle in completing the path was the old, narrow East Third Avenue bridge over Marina Lagoon. A new bridge was finished in 1987, allowing the old bridge to be saved for hikers and bicyclists.

As you ride south (winds are usually northwesterly), you'll pass under the massive steel towers of San Mateo Bridge.

Foster City was built around Brewer Island and 18 million cubic yards of landfill. Before the city was built, the island was part of a vast wetlands, which was gradually turned into salt ponds. The levees were built to keep out the bay water, and without them Foster City would be a marsh.

This planned community was the dream of Texas oil man T. Jack Foster and Bay Area businessman Richard Grant. In 1959 they purchased the island from the Schilling and Leslie Salt companies. Construction began after a lengthy battle by environmentalists opposed to filling in the Bay. A state bill was passed to create a municipal improvement district that would govern the city. By 1964, 200 families lived in Foster City. Today Foster City has 28,000 residents.

48 Sawyer Camp Trail

Distance: 11 miles
Terrain: Flat
Traffic: Bicyclists, hikers

Mileage Log

0.0 Start mileage at the south access, at the Skyline Boulevard and Crystal Springs Road intersection. Parking is available on Crystal Springs Road. 3.4 Water, toilets, picnic tables. Historic bay tree located 25 yards to west of tables. 5.0 Top of San Andreas Dam. 5.9 North entrance to Sawyer Camp Road at Hillcrest Boulevard. Return same way or you can take frontage road back to Sawyer Camp Road. Ride up the freeway ramp onto Interstate 280 heading south. (Yes, it's legal.) Stay on the walkway until ramp ends.

6.6 Take the Trousdale Drive exit. Immediately pick up the walkway.

6.7 Left on Trousdale Drive at stop sign.

6.8 Right on Skyline Boulevard at stop sign.

9.7 Right on Golf Course Road at stop sign, and ride under Interstate 280.

9.8 Left on Skyline Boulevard at stop sign.

11.1 Return to Sawyer Camp Trail.

Sawyer Camp Trail in San Mateo County isn't just popular, it's the Yosemite Park of recreation paths. As many as 1,300 visitors flock to the narrow, paved path along the east shore of Upper Crystal Springs Reservoir on a busy Sunday, more than 300,000 annually. The trail has another interesting distinction. It runs directly over the San Andreas Fault. Even without an earthquake, enjoying pristine blue reservoirs along the trail can be a "moving" experience.

Start riding from the south entrance. The eight-foot-wide path follows the east shore of Crystal Springs Reservoir. There's usually a refreshing breeze and shade from oaks, buckeyes, and tan oak. Restrooms and a drinking fountain are located on the trail 3.4 miles from the south entrance, with picnic tables nearby. A short distance off the trail, don't miss seeing one of the oldest and largest bay laurel trees in the state. The Jepson laurel was named in honor of Willis Jepson, a California botanist.

North of the picnic grounds, the trail passes fern-covered slopes and a grove of bay trees that give welcome shade on hot summer days. Springs and a creek keep the area green year-round. You'll have a gradual climb to San Andreas Dam, followed by a steeper climb to the north entrance at Hillcrest Boulevard. Retrace the path, or, if you're not bothered by cars, return on Skyline Boulevard as described in the Mileage Log.

The best time to ride the trail is midweek when there aren't so many people, but early mornings on weekends aren't bad either. Obey the posted 10 mph speed limit, and always slow for hikers. The Peninsula's water supply is closely monitored by

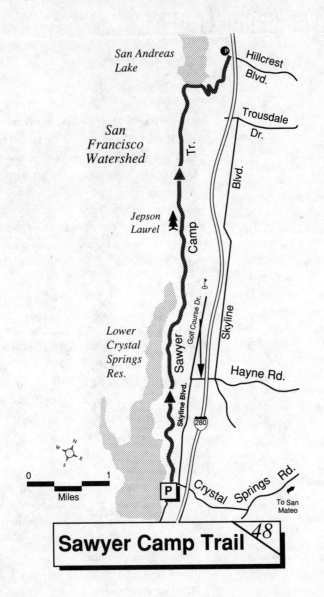

San Andreas
Lake

Hillcrest
Blvd.

San
Francisco
Watershed

Trousdale
Dr.

Jepson
Laurel

Lower
Crystal
Springs
Res.

Hayne Rd.

0   1
Miles

Crystal Springs Rd.

To San
Mateo

Sawyer Camp Trail *48*

the San Francisco Water Department; watershed land to the west of the reservoir is closed to the public.

Sawyer Camp Road was a little-used dirt road until 1979, when the county paved it. The road's history goes back to the 1850s. Leander Sawyer kept an inn here to serve picnickers and raise prize circus horses. The valley road later became the main stagecoach route from Millbrae to Half Moon Bay.

San Andreas Reservoir was built in 1869 to provide water for burgeoning San Francisco; in 1934, the Hetch Hetchy pipeline was built to bring water from the Tuolumne River in the High Sierra to San Andreas Lake and its neighboring dams to the south, Upper (1877) and Lower (1888) Crystal Springs reservoirs. All three dams withstood the 1906 earthquake. For more information, contact the San Mateo County Parks Department, (415) 363-4020.

49 Shoreline Park

Distance: 10 miles
Terrain: Flat
Traffic: Bicyclists, hikers

Mileage Log

0.0 Start mileage at entrance to Shoreline Park on Shoreline Boulevard. Ride north on recreation path. 1.1 Cross Permanente Creek and take first right. Right again in 50 yards on path. Portable toilets at intersection.

1.7 Right, followed by open gate.

1.9 Right on dirt levee at pump house and portable toilets. Levee heads into Bay and returns to Palo Alto.

4.4 Right on road at Palo Alto recycling center. Gate.

4.6 Straight at Embarcadero Road junction and stop sign. 5.1 Palo Alto Baylands Interpretive Center on left. Turn around and return by same road.

5.6 Right on Embarcadero Road at stop sign.

6.0 Left on Faber Place next to car dealership.

6.1 Right at end of Faber Place onto recreation path.

6.5 Left at frontage road, staying on recreation path.

8.0 Left on paved path immediately after crossing bridge over Adobe Creek.

Shoreline Park, like many parks bordering the Bay, is located on a former garbage dump. San Francisco buried its garbage here for more than 13 years. The city of Mountain View used the $13 million it raised in dumping fees to pay for the park. From the way it looks today, you'd never guess it was a dump. It's one of the premier parks on the Bay for casual riding.

The city got more than just a beautiful park from the arrangement. The ground is rich in methane, a byproduct of rotting garbage. The gas brings in $170,000 annually, enough to pay for park maintenance. The city capped off the lengthy shoreline development project in 1986 by opening Shoreline Amphitheatre, brainchild of the late Bill Graham. Top recording artists perform at the tent-shaped outdoor theater.

Most of the park offers a quiet, peaceful setting to be enjoyed while riding on recreation paths that skirt the Bay. In the park center there's a man-made lake with a boat launch, golf course, and clubhouse. In the fall, the salt ponds have some of the best duck watching anywhere in the Bay Area; the park interior has ring-necked pheasant and burrowing owls.

The ride starts from a parking lot inside the main entrance at the north end of Shoreline Boulevard and loops through Palo Alto baylands on salt pond levees. On the way to the levees you'll cross Permanente Creek on a wooden bridge. There's a pump house and a portable toilet where the dirt levee begins. Turn right and ride north to the Palo Alto dump on a dirt levee. (Beware: the levee turns to a quagmire in the rain.) The dump has been closed and will soon open as a city park.

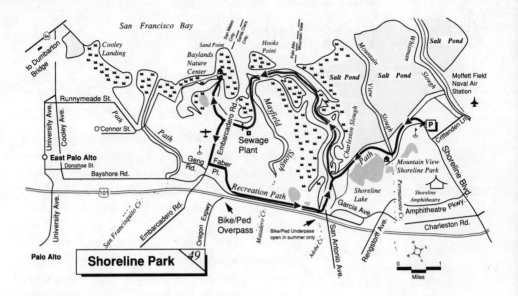

8.4 Right at pump house on recreation path.

8.6 Left at T intersection.

9.2 Left at junction and then left again to cross bridge over Permanente Creek.

10.3 End ride at park entrance.

From the dump, take a paved road, where there's a recycling center. Ride north to the Baylands Nature Center next to the airport. The center is built on concrete pilings over the salt marsh. It holds guided bike rides and walks, and presents slide shows, and movies about the Bay. Call (415) 329-2506 for a schedule.

Return to Embarcadero Road and turn right. Go 0.4 miles and turn left onto Faber Lane. Pick up the recreation path at the end of the street and head south. You'll cross Matadero Creek, Dry Creek, and then Adobe Creek before turning left to take the path back to the pump station. The marsh on your left was reclaimed in 1993 by the city of Palo Alto. A path that goes under Highway 101 next to Adobe Creek is open during the dry season. Turn right at the pump house and retrace your route. For more information about Shoreline Park, contact the city of Mountain View, P.O. Box 7540, Mountain View, CA 94039. Phone (415) 966-6392.

Casual Rides

50 Coyote Creek Trail

Distance: 30 miles round-trip
Terrain: Flat
Traffic: Bicyclists, hikers

Mileage Log

0.0 Hellyer Park Velodrome. Start mileage at beginning of path, next to restrooms.

0.2 Straight at junction with bridge. Cottonwood Lake on left. 0.8 Ride under Highway 101. 1.7 Reforestation. 2.3 Bridge on right.

2.9 Ride under new Piercy Avenue bridge. 3.0 Ride over old bridge and 3.1 turn left to continue trail. Coyote Creek on left. 5.5 Ride under Highway 101 (junction for new Highway 85). 5.8 Road turns to dirt. Weir on left. Continue straight on levy. 6.4 Begin new trail along Monterey highway.

6.7 Left on new recreation bridge, then immediate right.

6.8 Cross Metcalf Road to Coyote Ranch Road (next to power station), followed by immediate right onto path.

7.7 Left back onto Coyote Ranch Road.

7.9 Right back onto path next to dog training area. 9.6 Golf course. 10.6 Cross road to golf course. Coyote Creek on left since dog kennel. 11.3 Cross bridge. 12.6 Begin dirt road. Construction area for gravel pit. 13.2 Return to paved path. Model airplane club. 14.0 Ride under Highway 101.

Here's a 29.5-mile round-trip route completely on recreation paths! It's the longest ride on a recreation path in the Bay Area. You can start in south San Jose and ride to Morgan Hill, then retrace the route. Hellyer Park is a convenient location to start riding.

Begin riding from the Velodrome, Northern California's only racing track. The 336-meter concrete oval, built in 1962, is owned by Santa Clara County. Ed Steffani, a retired civil engineer from Los Gatos, designed and helped build the track. On Friday nights in the summer there's racing under the lights. But the crowds pale in comparison to San Jose track racing in the 1920s and 1930s, when gambling was legal.

The path follows Coyote Creek under the shade of cottonwoods, sycamores, and oaks. San Jose retains a public right-of-way along most of the creek's 31 miles. Plans call for extending the trail the length of Coyote Creek from Anderson Reservoir to San Francisco Bay.

The path dips under the Hellyer Avenue bridge and then passes Cottonwood Lake on the left. The lake is stocked with trout and bluegill, and there's a playground nearby for the kids. The eight-foot-wide trail follows Coyote Creek, normally placid, though it flooded in the early 1980s, wiping out a section of the trail.

Industrial parks can be seen everywhere along the trail, but Santa Clara Valley clings to a few parcels of its agricultural heritage nearby; orchards and vegetable fields mix with housing developments.

At 3.1 miles, ride under the new bridge and then turn right onto the old Piercy Road Bridge. Take an immediate left after crossing the bridge. The

Casual Rides

Coyote Creek Trail 50

14.7 Trail ends. Anderson Reservoir ranger station. Turn around and return same way.

29.5 Ride ends.

Above: The velodrome at Hellyer Park is the scene of weekend racing and training.

Below: Coyote Creek County Park's recreation path links the suburbs of San Jose with Morgan Hill.

trail picks up on the west side of the creek, winding through orchards and past farmhouses.

The paved trail ends at a weir. A dirt road continues for about half a mile to Monterey Highway, or you can continue right at the junction and stay on the paved path to Metcalf Road.

The newest stretch of 10-foot-wide path was finished in 1991 at a cost of $1 million and extends from a mile south of Metcalf Road to Anderson Reservoir ranger station. The trail crosses a bridge and skirts the edge of a golf course. Picnic benches are conveniently located at several locations on the path. There's another short section of dirt road (it will be paved) that passes a gravel pit. Watch for low-flying model airplanes beyond the gravel pit, where there's a popular airplane park.

Note that northwesterly winds can make the return trip a good deal more difficult.

Casual Rides

51 Los Gatos Creek Trail

Distance: 12 miles
Terrain: Flat
Traffic: Bicyclists, hikers

Mileage Log

0.0 Start ride at Vasona Park in Los Gatos. Begin mileage at Peppertree Lane and Los Gatos Creek at stop sign.

0.2 Keep left, following striped path next to Vasona Lake. 0.6 Restrooms on right. 1.0 Vasona Lake Dam on left.

1.6 Left on sidewalk, crossing Los Gatos Creek on the Lark Avenue bridge. Turn left after crossing the bridge to pick up trail below bridge. 1.7 Keep left riding through small park.

3.4 Ride under San Tomas Expressway and then cross Los Gatos Creek on wooden bridge at spillway. 4.5 Campbell Park on left at Campbell Avenue. 4.9 Pruneridge shopping center access on right. 5.4 San Jose Water Works at right on Bascom Avenue.

6.1 Path ends at Williams School. Return by same route.

12.2 End ride at Vasona Park.

Maybe someday the Los Gatos Creek Recreation Path will join the Coyote Creek Recreation Path, which will join the Bayshore Recreation Path, the Stevens Creek Recreation Path, the Guadalupe River Recreation Path, and so on until we no longer need to ride on city streets. We can only dream about it right now, and be content with a 6-mile path following Los Gatos Creek from Los Gatos to west San Jose.

Start the ride at Vasona County Park, just east of downtown Los Gatos. The park has a passenger-carrying miniature train, a historic carousel with lovingly restored antique horses, playgrounds, barbecue pits, food stands, a lake with ducks, and lots of grass. Parking is scarce on busy weekends.

The path follows Los Gatos Creek, which can be a roaring stream or a mud puddle, depending on whether or not water is being released from Lexington Reservoir. At the east end of Vasona Park, you'll ride around Vasona Lake dam, built in 1935 for flood control.

Farther along, you'll pass percolation ponds, a favorite gathering place for urban fishermen. A wide variety of waterfowl prefer the percolation ponds, everything from white-plumed egrets to coots. At the west edge of the percolation ponds, there's a creek crossing that leads to dirt trails. The new Highway 85 extension has made its presence felt: it now crosses the creek near Lark Avenue.

Continuing east, you'll pass Campbell Park on the left at the Campbell Avenue overpass. A Parcourse begins at the park and follows the Los Gatos trail. There's a 1-mile stretch of paved path on the other side of the creek next to a mobile home park. On weekends the trail is popular with walkers, joggers, and roller skaters.

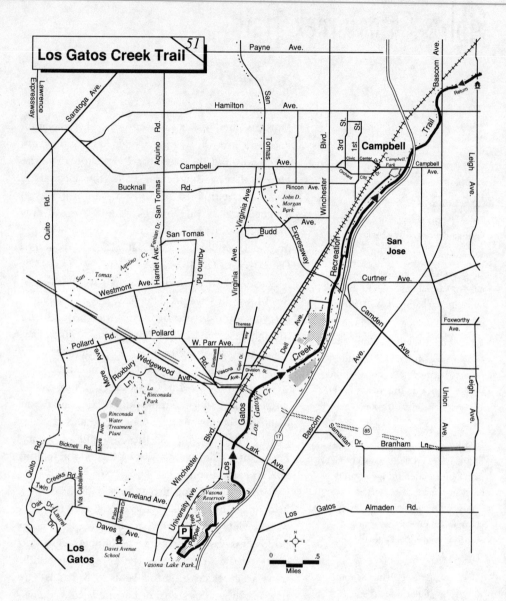

Los Gatos Creek Trail

51

Payne Ave.

Lawrence Expressway

Saratoga Ave.

Aquino Rd.

Quito Rd.

Hamilton Ave.

San Tomas Ave.

Bascom Ave.

Trail

Return

Campbell Ave.

Campbell

3rd St.

1st St.

Civic Center

Campbell Park

Orchard

City Dr.

Campbell Ave.

Leigh Ave.

Bucknall Rd.

Winchester Blvd.

Rincon Ave.

John D. Morgan Bgrk

Budd Ave.

San Jose

San Tomas

Fenian Dr.

Harriet Ave.

San Tomas

Aquino Cr.

San Tomas

Westmont Ave.

Aquino Rd.

Virginia Ave.

Virginia Ave.

Expressway

Recreation

Curtner Ave.

Camden Ave.

Foxworthy Ave.

Pollard Rd.

Pollard

Theresa

Dell

Creek

Ave.

Pollard Rd.

More Ave.

Roxbury Ln.

Wedgewood Ave.

W. Parr Ave.

Dardenelli Ln.

Vasona Ave.

Cleon Dr.

hwy

Division St.

Los Gatos Cr.

Bascom

Union Ave.

Leigh Ave.

La Rinconada Park

Gatos Blvd.

17

Samaritan Dr.

85

Branham Ln.

Rinconada Water Treatment Plant

Lark Ave.

Quito Rd.

Bicknell Rd.

More Ave.

Twin Creeks Rd.

Via Caballero

Vineland Ave.

University Ave.

Winchester Blvd.

Los Gatos Blvd.

Vasona Reservoir

Los Gatos

Almaden Rd.

Oak Dr.

Laurel Dr.

Palos Verdes Dr.

Daves Ave.

P

Pepper Ln.

Los Gatos

Daves Avenue School

Vasona Lake Park

W — E
N
S

0 .5
Miles

Bibliography

Anderson, Charles. *Mountain Bike Trails of the Bay Area.* Palo Alto, Calif.: Omega Printing, 1984.

Arrigoni, Patricia. *Making the Most of Marin: A California Guide.* Novato, Calif.: Presidio Press, 1981.

Beal, Richard A. *Highway 17.* Aptos, Calif.: The Pacific Group, 1991.

Butler, Phyllis Filiberti. *The Valley of Santa Clara: Historic Buildings, 1792–1920.* San Jose, Calif.: Junior League of San Jose, 1975.

Danville, Portrait of 125 Years. Town of Danville. Alamo, Calif.: Robert Pease & Co.

Davis, Dorothy. *A Pictorial History of Pleasanton.* Pleasanton, Calif.: Pleasanton National Bicentennial Committee, 1976.

Emmanuels, George. *California's Contra Costa County: An Illustrated History.* Fresno, Calif.: Panorama West Books, 1986.

Futcher, Jane. *Marin, the Place the People: Profile of a California County.* New York: Holt, Reinhart, and Winston, 1981.

Geologic Guidebook of the San Francisco Bay Counties. San Francisco: State of California, Division of Mines, 1951.

Graves, Al, and Ted Wurm. *The Crookedest Railroad in the World.* Glendale, Calif.: Trans-Anglo Books, 1983.

Halley, William. *The Centennial Year Book of Alameda County.* Oakland, Calif.

Hynding, Alan. *From Frontier to Suburb: The Story of San Mateo Peninsula.* Belmont, Calif.: Star Publishing, 1982.

Kneiss, Gilbert H. *Redwood Railways.* San Diego: Howell-North Press, 1956.

Koch, Margaret. *Santa Cruz County: Parade of the Past.* Fresno, Calif.: Valley Publishers, 1973.

Lewis, Oscar. *San Francisco: Mission to Metropolis.* San Diego: Howell-North Books, 1966.

MacGregor, Bruce, and Richard Truesdale. *A Centennial: South Pacific Coast.* Boulder, Colo.: Pruett Publishing, 1982.

McCarthy, Frances Florence. *The History of Mission San Jose California 1779–1835.* Fresno, Calif.: Academy Library Guild, 1958.

Neumann, Phyllis. *Sonoma County Bike Trails.* Penngrove, Calif.: 1978.

O'Hare, Carol. *A Bicyclist's Guide to Bay Area History.* Sunnyvale, Calif.: Fair Oaks Publishing, 1989.

Payne, Stephen M. *Santa Clara County: Harvest of Change.* Northridge, Calif.: Windsor Publications, 1987.

Richards, Gilbert. *Crossroads, People and Events of the Redwoods of San Mateo County.* Woodside, Calif.: Gilbert Richards Publications, 1973.

Sandoval, John. *The History of Washington Township.* Castro Valley, Calif.: 1985.

Stanger, Frank M. *Sawmills in the Redwoods: Logging on the San Francisco Peninsula, 1849–1967.* San Mateo, Calif.: San Mateo County Historical Association, 1967.

Stanger, Frank M. *South from San Francisco: San Mateo County, California, Its History and Heritage.* San Mateo, Calif.: San Mateo County Historical Association, 1963.

Tays, George, ed. *Historical Landmarks and Sites of Alameda County, California.* Oakland, Calif.: Alameda County Library, 1938.

Verardo, Denzil, and Jennie Dennis. *Napa Valley: From Golden Fields to Purple Harvest.* Northridge, Calif.: Windsor Publications, 1986.

Whitnah, Dorothy L. *An Outdoor Guide to the San Francisco Bay Area.* Berkeley, Calif.: Wilderness Press, 1976.

Young, John V. *Ghost Towns of the Santa Cruz Mountains.* Santa Cruz, Calif.: Western Tanager Press, 1984.

Index

About the Author

Ray Hosler rides his bicycle as a way of life, whether it be for commuting, for riding to the store to buy a loaf of bread, or for recreation. He has ridden his bicycle through the Alps, in Thailand, and in many parts of California and Colorado. He is a former bicycle columnist for the *San Francisco Chronicle* and currently writes for a computer company in Silicon Valley.